# The Impossible Faith

*Why Christianity Succeeded*
*When It Should Have Failed*

James Patrick Holding

*The Impossible Faith*
by James Patrick Holding

Printed in the United States of America

ISBN 978-1-60266-084-7



Unless otherwise indicated, Bible quotations are taken from the King James Version of the Bible.

www.xulonpress.com

# *Table of Contents*

# *Preface:*

# *A Thesis So Explosive, An Atheist Paid Over $5,000 for An Answer To It*

"Christianity is no different than any other religion." The record of history belies such a simple statement, and makes it clear that most systems of faith, unlike Christianity, do not survive or thrive, but end up either dead or drastically altered. Social, theological, and historical pressures inevitably come to bear and force most religious faiths to either change with the times or cease to exist.

*The Impossible Faith* offers an explosive proposition: That Christianity, by the reckoning of men, ought to have been one of those faiths that either passed into history or became seriously altered. The ancient world did not share our modern values, and the social, religious, and philosophical conditions in which Christianity was founded and grew were antithetical, in every conceivable way, to its message. In contrast, the Christian faith had none of the advantages that other thriving faiths, such as Islam and Mormonism, had during their formative years. There is simply no possibility that Christianity could have been accepted by anyone in the ancient world, unless its first missionaries had indisputable proof and testimony of the faith's central tenet, the resurrection of Jesus Christ. Had there not been such indisputable evidence to present, Christianity would have been an impossible faith.

In this book, we will lay out four primary social and historical factors that will demonstrate the impossibility of Christianity in the eyes of the people of the first century, and offer a positive apologetic for the Christian faith and the resurrection of Jesus Christ. Christian readers will be encouraged and emboldened by the message of *The Impossible Faith*, as they realize, from a new perspective, "how firm a foundation" they have in Christ Jesus. Non-Christian readers who encounter *The Impossible Faith* will be challenged to consider the truth of Christianity in a new light.

The arguments made in this book are so powerful that one atheist reader paid another atheist over *five thousand dollars* to write a response to them. Can you afford not to give them consideration ?

# *The Mistaken Messiah*

*Matthew 24:5 For many shall come in my name, saying, I am Christ; and shall deceive many.*

Journey with me, if you will, to a time of great anticipation and excitement. The year is 1666, and the place is Adrianople, in what is now Turkey. A man is making his way through the streets of the city, on his way to the palace of the Islamic sultan. His name is Sabbatai Sevi, and he is the long-awaited Jewish *Messiah.*

Sabbatai Sevi, an eccentric ascetic with a fondness for mysticism, first expressed his messianic ambitions almost fifteen years prior to his visit to Adrianople. His words and deeds kindled hopes among the minority Jewish populations in Europe, Western Asia, Palestine, and North Africa that the day would soon come when they would no longer suffer the insults, abuses, and persecution of their Christian and Muslim neighbors. Sevi offered a messianic campaign rooted in mystical interpretations of the Jewish scriptures, ecstatic visions and prophecies, and, so it was rumored, manifestations of miraculous power. All across the land, Jewish families praised the God of their fathers for the coming of the Messiah — the one who would finally vindicate Israel!

As the Messiah made his way to the sultan's palace, there was a buzz of excitement among the Jews of Adrianople, and a firm belief that Sevi was on his way to take the sultan's crown and place it on his own head. "Before long," one brash young Jewish man said to a visiting Frenchman, "you will be our slaves by the power of the messiah!" Sevi entered the sultan's palace, and the doors closed behind him. The entire Jewish population waited, breathless, for the trumpet of messianic triumph.

There are numerous and varied accounts of what happened on that day in September, 1666, when Sevi appeared before the sultan's council. However, all agree upon the end result, an event which one historian calls "one of the most tragic moments in Jewish history." Sabbatai Sevi did not take the sultan's crown that day. Instead, in a shocking and inexplicable reversal, Sabbatai Sevi emerged from that meeting as a new convert to Islam, holding as his reward a minor, honorary position as a gatekeeper in the sultan's palace. The one who would be the Messiah had instead become an apostate!

Over the next two years, the Jews that had come to believe in Sevi's messiahship came to grips with his apostasy. Many forsook his movement at once. Some converted to Christianity or Islam. Some asserted that Sevi had apostasized in order to test their faith in him. Others saw it as a ploy for Sevi to learn the secrets of the sultan's palace, in order to overthrow the sultan later. Still others declared that Sevi had actually ascended to heaven, and it was only an illusion of Sevi that had committed apostasy. Others yet put a positive "spin" on the matter: Sevi had performed the role of Messiah unerringly, for in apostasizing, he had saved the Jewish nation from destruction by mollifying an enemy of the Jews.

Sevi lived for another ten years, at first helping convert other Jews to Islam, then showing some signs of reversing his apostasy. At that point the sultan acted again, banishing Sevi to what is now Albania and keeping him in isolation. After Sevi's death, one of his followers declared that within the next twelve months, Sevi would reappear, and this time he would *really* mean business. The twelve months passed. Sevi remained buried. [1]

The Sabbatian messianic movement did not die out completely. Even to this day, a handful of Sabbatians live on in Istanbul as a mystical, half-Jewish, half-Islamic sect called the Domne. However, the history of the Sabbatian movement reveals a fundamental truth about social and religious movements: The bolder they get in their claims and demands, the harder it becomes for them to survive when times of trial come upon them. How well such movements can meet their challenges will determine how, and in what form, they will continue to exist, if at all.

Some religious movements survive by making their claims inaccessible to criticism. A religion that makes claims that are solely philosophical or mystical in nature takes few risks of being criticized or disproved. Other religious movements "move the goalposts" by changing their doctrines when they come under fire. Many religious movements end up either dead, nearly dead, or drastically altered. Social, theological, and historical pressures inevitably come to bear and force most religious faiths to either change with the times or cease to exist. The smoldering testimony of the Branch Davidian compound, and the suicide victims of the Heaven's Gate comet cult, are effective witnesses to the worst that can happen when a religious movement with neither a firm foundation nor a theological escape hatch comes face to face with hostile realities.

Our thesis is a provocative one: That Christianity, by the reckoning of men, ought to have been one of those faiths, like the Sabbatean movement or the comet cult, that either largely passed into history or became seriously altered. In the following chapters we will draw together several social and historical factors affecting early Christianity, and challenge the reader to consider the truth of the Christian faith in a new light, concluding with the proposition that Christianity was, indeed, an "impossible faith."

## Note

[1] Information on Sabbatai Sevi is derived from Gershom Scholem, *Sabbatai Sevi: The Mystical Messiah* (Princeton: Princeton University Press, 1973); 207, 673-693, 754-760, 792-3, 882, 920.

# *A Prophet Without Honor*

*Mark 6:4 A prophet is not without honour, but in his own country, and among his own kin, and in his own house.*

"Do the honorable thing." When we say this, we mean "do what is right." "Honorable," however, is not a synonym for "right." "Honor" refers to how we are perceived in the eyes of others. The opposite of "honorable" is not "wrong," but "shameful."

In a culture like that of medieval Japan, a *samurai* warrior might commit suicide because he had been embarrassed, and dishonored. Few today in America (or in the Western world) would sanction suicide for such reasons. To us, loss of honor is seldom earth-shattering, and is often met with defensive indifference. But the people who lived in the time of the Bible would not have reacted as we do to a loss of honor. That which was honorable was, to these peoples, of primary importance. "The promise of honor and threat of disgrace [were] prominent goads to pursue a certain kind of life and to avoid many alternatives."[1] Honor was placed above one's personal safety and was the key element in deciding courses of action. Shame and honor were the leading social motivators for the people of the Bible, and it was not an option to hold one's head high in defiance and tell others to mind their own business.

How does this ancient focus on honor make Christianity an "impossible faith"? Try to remember what you thought when you first saw a depiction of Jesus on the cross. Most of us probably responded with sympathy. A few of us may have wondered at the seeming contradiction of God descending as a man and enduring such treatment.

If it makes little sense to us, it made much less sense to the people of the New Testament era, because in their eyes, to be crucified was to suffer the *most dishonorable* form of execution possible. Crucifixion was "known as an intentionally degrading death, fixing the criminal's honor at the lowest end of the spectrum and serving as an effective deterrent to others, reminding them of the shameful end that awaits those who similarly deviate from the dominant culture's values."[2] The early Christians knew that preaching a savior who underwent this disgraceful treatment was folly in the eyes of Jews and Gentiles alike. "For the preaching of the cross is to them that perish foolishness..." (1 Corinthians 1:18; cf. Hebrews 12:2) "Cursed is every one that hangeth on a tree!" (Galatians 3:13) Paul is quoting Deuteronomy 21:23, which referred in its original context to the practice of executing someone and *then* hanging their bodies from a tree. But by the time of Jesus, the Jews had applied this verse to crucifixion. Any Jew who was crucified by the Romans would have been seen as subjected to the curses of Deuteronomy, promised by God to any person who was disobedient. The one the Christians claimed was the Son of God was subjected to the punishment and disgrace of those who rejected God!

What others thought of crucifixion, and of the Christians' crucified savior, makes it clear how significant this hurdle was for the Christian faith. The Jewish historian Josephus described crucifixion as "the most wretched of deaths." The second-century Christian apologist Justin Martyr wrote that the pagans "...say that our madness consists in the fact that we put a crucified man in second place after the unchangeable and eternal God..." The pagan writer and critic of Christianity, Celsus, described Jesus as one who was "bound in the most ignominious fashion" and "executed in a shameful way." An oracle of Apollo described Jesus as "a god who died in delusions... executed in the prime of life by the worst of deaths, a death bound with iron [nails]." The Biblical scholar Walter Bauer rightly said:

> *The enemies of Christianity always referred to the disgracefulness of the death of Jesus with great emphasis and malicious pleasure. A god or son of god dying on a cross! That was enough to put paid to the new religion.*[3]

If Jesus had truly been a god, then by ancient thinking, the crucifixion should never have happened, or at least somehow been negated, perhaps by Jesus disappearing suddenly from the cross. Near the end of the first century some Christian converts felt the pressure of such thinking and adopted a belief called *docetism* — the heresy that Jesus was not human at all, but an illusion. Mainstream Christianity argued that Jesus' death was an honorable act of sacrifice for the good of all men, as a soldier might die on the battlefield to save the lives of others.[4] But that sort of argument only works if you are already convinced by other means that what Jesus did was honorable. Why, then, were there any Christians at all?

At best, Christianity should have been a movement that had only a few Jewish followers, then died out within decades. The historical reality of the crucifixion could not be denied. To survive, Christianity should have either turned to docetism wholeheartedly, or else not bothered with Jesus at all, or merely made him into the movement's first martyr for a higher moral ideal within Judaism.

The disgrace of the crucifixion was the greatest shame that Jesus endured for our sake, but it was far from the only dishonor he bore. The Jewish officials who slapped Jesus' face and challenged "Prophesy!" were delivering calculated insults to Jesus' personal honor by challenging his claim to be a prophet. The Roman soldiers who dressed Jesus in robes and a crown of thorns, and then mocked him, were negating Jesus' honor and his claim to be King of the Jews. By the thinking of an honor-based society, Jesus should have met the challenges and shown himself to be a true prophet or king.[5] As Celsus sarcastically asked, "Why did this son of a god not show one glimmer of his divinity under these conditions? Why did he refuse to deliver himself from shame—at least play the man and stand up for his own or his father's honor?"[6]

The criminal charges brought against Jesus were also dishonorable. Do you know someone who has a police record and is ashamed of it? By the thinking of his contemporaries, Jesus openly committed blasphemy and pled guilty to sedition against the Roman state. "Those who elected to follow such a subversive and disgraced man were immediately suspect in the eyes of [Jews and Romans]."[7] Celsus asked, "If [Jesus] was a god, is it likely that he would have run away? Would he have permitted himself to be arrested?"[8] Would you pledge spiritual and eternal allegiance to a man with a prominent "rap sheet"?

Finally, the burial of Jesus was dishonorable. Does that seem surprising? The Gospels tell us that Joseph of Arimathea was a follower of Jesus, and a just and righteous man. But no matter how good Joseph's intentions were, for Jesus to be buried in Joseph's tomb, and not in a tomb belonging to Jesus' own family, was distinctly dishonorable.[9]

How could a man, subject to such overwhelming disgrace, in a society where honor was so crucial, have come to be recognized as the Son of God? There is only one viable explanation: Christianity succeeded because from the cross came victory, and after death came resurrection and vindication. As Biblical scholar David deSilva rightly puts it:

> *No member of the Jewish community or the Greco-Roman society would have come to faith or joined the Christian movement without first accepting that God's perspective on what kind of behavior merits honor differs exceedingly from the perspective of human beings, since the message about Jesus is that both the Jewish and Gentile leaders of Jerusalem evaluated Jesus, his convictions and his deeds as meriting a shameful death, but God overturned their evaluation of Jesus by raising him from the dead and seating him at God's own right hand as Lord.* [10]

The shame of the cross, Christianity's most enormous stumbling block, turns out to be one of its most incontrovertible proofs. Without solid evidence of the vindication of Jesus, Christianity would have been an "impossible faith" for anyone to believe.

## Notes

[1] David A. deSilva, *Honor, Patronage, Kinship, and Purity* (Downers Grove, Ill.: InterVarsity Press, 2000), 24.

[2] deSilva, 51.

[3] Ibid.

[4] deSilva, 52.

[5] deSilva, 31-2.

[6] R. Joseph Hoffmann, trans. *Celsus: On the True Doctrine* (New York: Oxford University Press, 1987), 65.

[7] deSilva, 46.

[8] Hoffmann, 61.

[9] Byron R. McCane, " 'Where No One Had Yet Been Laid': The Shame of Jesus' Burial," in B.D. Chilton and C.A. Evans (eds.), *Authenticating the Activities of Jesus* (NTTS, 28.2; Leiden: E.J. Brill, 1998), 431-452. McCane believes that Joseph was not really a disciple of Jesus, just a Sanhedrin member doing his duty as a member of the political body which had condemned Jesus, and was obliged to provide for some sort of burial. We would suggest that Joseph used such a duty as a pretext to get hold of Jesus' body before another Sanhedrin member with less respect for Jesus did so. The amount of spices brought by Nicodemus, which McCane finds "problematic," is easily interpreted as an attempt by devoted and wealthy disciples like Joseph and Nicodemus to add some small honor to an unavoidably dishonorable burial.

[10] deSilva, 51.

# *Politically Incorrect*

*Titus 1:12b The Cretians are alway liars, evil beasts, slow bellies.*

Take the word "Cretians" out of the above verse and substitute any ethnic or religious designation of your choice. Does that seem offensive? In modern America, a statement like Titus 1:12 would raise a cry of discontent from the group designated "liars and beasts." Had he said such a thing in public in our day, Paul would have been heckled from his podium, and perhaps physically assaulted. Activist groups with names like the Cretian Anti-Defamation League would have been formed. Lawsuits would have been filed. Paul would have been fired from his job or remanded for sensitivity training. He may have even been compelled to visit Cretian public forums and apologize to the Cretians he had offended.

But ancient Rome was not modern America. The ancients would not have turned to political activism, nor would they have remanded Paul for his words.

Indeed, the poet that Paul quotes, Epiminides, was himself a Cretian saying this about his fellow Cretians! Say today that a racial or ethnic group is composed of liars and beasts, and you will have half a dozen civil rights groups ringing your doorbell. Say it in Rome and you'd have everyone agreeing with you – including, sometimes, the group itself!

Have you ever noticed that the New Testament is filled with personal descriptions which specify what city, nation, or ethnic group a person is from? We read past such designations as "Jesus of Nazareth" or "Lydia of Thyatira" (Acts 16:14) without a second thought. But in the ancient world, persons were readily identified in terms of where they were from and from whom they were descended, and these identifications were assumed to give important information about them. To put it in modern terms, the ancient world believed in and accepted as valid what we call *stereotypes*. These prejudices of the ancient world seem silly and fanciful to us. But they formed an important part of an ancient person's perception of others, in a way that also made Christianity an "impossible faith."

Jesus already had "three strikes" against him with respect to widely-held ancient prejudices and stereotypes. There was no escaping these stereotypes, and no getting around them by saying, "You shouldn't judge a man by his race or national origin. You should consider his teachings."[1] The ancients did not concentrate on the individual, but on the group, and to be a member of a group was to share "a virtual identity with the group as a whole and its other members."[2]

**Strike #1: Jesus the Jew.** The identity of Jesus as a Jewish prophet was a major impediment to spreading the Gospel beyond the Jews themselves. Judaism as a religion was regarded by the Romans and Gentiles as a *superstition*, a false religion that undermined the social order of the Roman Empire because of its significantly different values and beliefs. Those who believed in superstitions, according to the Romans, bucked the established cosmic order, and their view of the universe was regarded as capricious and irrational. To appease the Roman gods meant to ensure the health and well being of Rome. To refuse to appease the Roman gods meant wishing Rome out of business.

This does not mean that some ancient writers did not have positive things to say about Judaism, or that as a religion it was unappreciated. Many found Judaism's ethical message attractive, and some became converts, or "God-fearers" like Cornelius (Acts 10:2). However, many Romans associated Judaism with a "standoffishness" that was actually the faithful Jew's way of strictly adhering to the commandments of the Bible.

Here is what the Roman historian Tacitus had to say about the Jewish people:

> *In order to secure the allegiance of his people in the future, Moses prescribed for them a novel religion quite different from those of the rest of mankind. Among the Jews all things*

*are profane that we hold sacred; on the other hand they regard as permissible what seems to us immoral...We are told that the seventh day was set aside for rest because this marked the end of their toils. In course of time the seductions of idleness made them devote every seventh year to indolence as well...*

*...The other practices of the Jews are sinister and revolting, and have entrenched themselves by their very wickedness. Wretches of the most abandoned kind who had no use for the religion of their fathers took to contributing dues and free-will offerings to swell the Jewish exchequer; and other reasons for their increasing wealth way be found in their stubborn loyalty and ready benevolence towards brother Jews. But the rest of the world they confront with the hatred reserved for enemies. They will not feed or intermarry with gentiles. Though a most lascivious people, the Jews avoid sexual intercourse with women of alien race. Among themselves nothing is barred. They have introduced the practice of circumcision to show that they are different from others. Proselytes to Jewry adopt the same practices, and the very first lesson they learn is to despise the gods, shed all feelings of patriotism, and consider parents, children and brothers as readily expendable...the Jewish belief is paradoxical and degraded.*[3]

So it is that bringing a Jewish savior to the door of the average Roman would have been a difficult task. If Christianity didn't have something special to offer, the Jewishness of Jesus *even by itself* means that the new faith should never have expanded in the Gentile world much beyond the circle of those Gentiles who were already Gentile proselytes to Judaism, like Cornelius.

**Strike #2: Jesus the Galilean.** Mention the land of *Galilee* to a Roman, and the effect would have been the same as saying "Iraq" or "Afghanistan" today. The Jewish historian Josephus said that Galileans "from childhood were trained for war" and his reports show that Galilee "produced the most notorious leaders of the [Jewish] fight against Rome."[4] The Galileans were renowned as fighters. Admitting that Jesus was a Galilean would immediately raise the suspicion that he was "up to no good" against the Roman state. Admitting further that Jesus had suffered crucifixion, the death of rebels against Rome, would confirm that opinion even further!

Among the Jews, the Galileans had another reputation: they were "presumed to be ignoramuses,"[5] especially on religious matters. In rabbinic literature after the time of the New Testament, "noted Galilean rabbinic figures are depicted as ignoring or neglecting the code of conduct binding on the sages," and the Galileans themselves were seen as having "a lack of familiarity with the sophisticated understanding and practice of the Torah."[6] One rabbinic account tells of a great teacher who spent 18 years trying to tutor the Galileans, only to leave in frustration with the hyperbolic assessment that the Galileans hated the Jewish law.

Galileans were also routinely made fun of for their way of speaking. "Surely thou art one of them: for thou art a Galilaean, and thy speech agreeth thereto." (Mark 14:70b) Galilean pronunciation was "notoriously slipshod"[7] and a distinctive mark of the Galilean people. Can we imagine the difficulty Jesus and his Apostles would have had preaching the Good News when everyone was laughing at their manner of speech?

**Strike #3: Jesus of Nazareth**. "...Paul said, I am a man which am a Jew of Tarsus, a city in Cilicia, a citizen of no mean city..." (Acts 21:39) When Paul mentioned that he was from Tarsus, it was not just friendly conversation! Being from a major city like Tarsus signified a high honor rating for the person who laid claim to it, and Paul needed his high rating to convince the Roman soldier that he was not just some ordinary rabble-rouser causing trouble. Christianity had another serious handicap in this regard: A savior from a puny village of no account. "And Nathanael said unto him, Can there any good thing come out of Nazareth?" (John 1:46) Jews and Gentiles alike would have scoffed at the notion that someone as important as the Messiah would have come from or lived in Nazareth! Surely he would reside in Jerusalem, or stay in Bethlehem where he was born; or at the very least, if Galilee had to be his home, then he should have been from the cosmopolitan city of Sepphoris, not four miles from Nazareth.

Ethnically and geographically, Jesus was everything that everyone did *not* expect a Messiah to be.

Thus everything about Jesus as a person was all wrong to get people to believe he was the Son of the Living God — and there must have been something powerful, like the resurrection, to overcome the stigmas of ancient stereotyping.

## Notes

[1] As Malina and Neyrey write of such attitudes in the ancient world, "One is never expected to question these prejudgments, and given social experience, even contrary evidence is selectively overlooked or considered nonexistent because it is absolutely impossible..." Thus for example to a Jew, "good Samaritan" would have been an oxymoron. 169.

[2] Ibid., 158.

[3] Tacitus, *Histories* 5.2-5. Taken from http://www.livius.org/am-ao/antisemitism/antisemitism-t.html

[4] Geza Vermes, *The Changing Faces of Jesus* (New York: Viking Compass, 2001), 241.

[5] Ibid., 244.

[6] Ibid., 243, 244. Jesus' Galilean origins also served to confuse those who would not have known of his birthplace in Bethlehem: "Others said, This is the Christ. But some said, Shall Christ come out of Galilee?...Search, and look: for out of Galilee ariseth no prophet." (John 7:41, 52b)

[7] Ibid., 243.

# *Physical Fitness*

*1 Corinthians 15:17 And if Christ be not raised, your faith is vain; ye are yet in your sins.*

*Acts 17:18b ...[They said,] He seemeth to be a setter forth of strange gods: because he preached unto them Jesus, and the resurrection.*

Paul's words to the Corinthian church express the core of the Christian faith: Christ was raised. By "raised" Paul means that Jesus was *resurrected.* Jesus did not return as a ghost or a spirit, but his *body* was raised from death and gloriously brought back to life.

Resurrection was a uniquely Jewish idea.[1] The blunt physicality of resurrection is made clear in several Old Testament passages and in Jewish works prior to and during the period of the New Testament.[2] Most Jews believed that at the end of history, all men would be resurrected and judged.[3] So, when Christianity taught that Jesus had been resurrected, this was strange to Jewish ears, because no one conceived of the idea of one *unique* resurrection before the time of final judgment. Still, the idea of an early, single resurrection would not have been an insurmountable obstacle in preaching to the Jews, as long as there was sufficient evidence to prove that it had happened.

On the other hand, the Resurrection was a major stumbling block in preaching to the Gentiles, for resurrection was a profoundly offensive concept which ran counter to Gentile philosophical thinking. The conventional wisdom of that day regarded matter as evil, and the physical body as the source of all of our problems. The best hope was for us to *get rid of* our body, not desire for it to be raised again![4] The resurrection of Jesus would have been regarded with scorn, and to be resurrected, as the Christian faith promised to believers, was an undesirable goal.

The pagan critic of Judaism and Christianity, Celsus, said of resurrection: "The soul may have everlasting life, but corpses, as Heraclitus said, 'ought to be thrown away as worse than dung'." The Roman writer Plutarch said it was "against nature" to "send bodies to heaven" and that only pure souls "cast no shadows" (i.e., had no bodies). The Romans used cremation to dispose of their dead, because "[t]he funeral pyre was said to burn away the body so that the immortal part could ascend to the gods."[5] In the Greco-Roman view, "man's highest good consisted of emancipation from corporeal defilement. The nakedness of disembodiment was the ideal state."[6] The reaction of the Athenians to Paul preaching the resurrection is revealing: "And when they heard of the resurrection of the dead, some mocked: and others said, We will hear thee again of this matter." (Acts 17:32) The first reaction, mockery, is exactly what we would expect from most Greeks. The second reaction is little more encouraging. At best, it indicates a desire to hear more about a strange teaching at a later date. At worst, it is the same as saying, "Don't call us, we'll call you!" Clearly, resurrection was the *last* sort of destiny for mankind that should have been preached in the Gentile world. Resurrection conflicted with the deepest convictions of the Gentiles about the nature of life after death, and about the ability of the divine to interact with the physical world. God could hardly even be believed to have been incarnated, much less resurrected! Christianity would have had a much easier time winning Gentile converts had it taught that Jesus' body was an illusion, or had been taken up to heaven, like Elijah's. This would have been a suitable match for the Roman view of the immortality of the soul, and the belief that the greatest men achieved *apotheosis*, or exaltation to divine rank, after death. So why make the road harder? How could converts have overcome these implacable reservations? There is only one plausible answer: Christianity really had a resurrection to preach, and solid evidence that a resurrection had taken place. Otherwise, Christian preaching and faith was in vain.

## Notes

[1] Some have argued that resurrection was taught within the Zoroastrian religion, and that the Jews may have even stolen the idea from Zoroastrianism. However, there is little evidence to support this thesis, and scholars of Zoroastrianism are split on the issue. See Edwin Yamauchi, *Persia and the Bible* (Grand Rapids: Baker, 1990), 461.

[2] In the Old Testament see Daniel 12:2-3, Ezekiel 37:1-12, and Isaiah 26:19, as well as John 5:25-29 in the New Testament. Other Jewish texts include 4 Ezra 7:32 ("The earth shall restore those who sleep in her, and the dust those who rest in it, and the chambers those entrusted to them."), 1 Enoch 51:1 ("In those days, the earth will also give back what has been entrusted to it, and Sheol [the underworld] will give back what it has received, and hell will give back what it owes."), and 2 Baruch 50:2 ("For certainly the earth will then restore the dead. It will not change their form, but just as it received them, so it will restore them.").

[3] The Sadducees were a notable exception, believing that there was no afterlife at all; see Matt. 22:23, Mark 12:18, and Luke 20:27.

[4] Pheme Perkins, *Resurrection: New Testament Witness and Contemporary Reflection* (New York: Doubleday, 1984), 61, states: "Christianity's pagan critics generally viewed resurrection as misunderstood metempsychosis at best. At worst, it seemed ridiculous."

[5] Edwin Yamauchi, "Life, Death, and Afterlife in the Ancient Near East," in *Life in the Face of Death: The Resurrection Message of the New Testament*, Richard N. Longenecker, ed. (Grand Rapids: Eerdmans, 1998), 73.

[6] Murray Harris, *Raised Immortal* (Grand Rapids: Eerdmans, 1983), 116.

# *Upending the Establishment*

*Acts 17:6 And when they found them not, they drew Jason and certain brethren unto the rulers of the city, crying, These that have turned the world upside down are come hither also...*

If someone comes knocking on your door claiming to have found a new and better religion, would you believe them? Would you give them a hearing? Most of us would politely decline to listen to such spiritual salesmen, but for many people, the desire for novelty in life, especially in religion, offers a powerful attraction. The proliferation of unusual religions such as the Heaven's Gate cult, attest to our desire for variety and uniqueness in religious contexts. Some of us are even willing to give our lives merely to be different.

The ancient world offers yet another contrast in this regard. Contemporary literature tells us that for people in the time of Jesus, "(t)he primary test of truth in religious matters was custom and tradition, the practices of the ancients."[1] If your beliefs had the right sort of background, and had been around long enough, you had the respect of the Romans. Otherwise, your beliefs were viewed with suspicion. For the Romans and other people who lived at the time of Jesus, old was good. Innovation was bad.

This was a significant problem for Christianity, because the faith could only trace its roots back to a recent founder. Christians were regarded as "arrogant innovators"[2] who, though their religion had appeared very recently, had the nerve to insist that believing in their new religion, and accepting their new prophet Jesus — whom, as we saw in Chapter 1, had been determined by the political powers of the age to have been worthy of death — was the only way to escape judgment. How arrogant to claim that the powers who judged Jesus worthy of the worst and most shameful sort of death were 180 degrees off, and God Himself said so! How much more arrogant to say that he offered a new religion that totally contradicted, and was superior to, all others that had been believed for centuries!

As Biblical scholars Bruce Malina and Jerome Neyrey[3] explain, among ancient Mediterranean peoples, reverence was given to ancestors, who were considered greater merely "by the fact of birth." People in this time and place "were culturally constrained to attempt the impossible task of living up to the traditions of those necessarily greater personages of their shared past." What had been handed down was "... presumed valid and normative. Forceful arguments might be phrased as: 'We have always done it this way!'" As the Romans put it, *Semper, ubique, ab omnibus* — "Always, everywhere, by everyone!" (In contrast, Christianity said, "Not any longer, not here, and not by us!") The Roman sentiment was especially held to be true where religion was concerned. Change or novelty in religious doctrine or practice met with an especially violent reaction, for change was "a means value which serve[d] to innovate or subvert core and secondary values."[4] Christian eschatology especially stood against a particularly significant perception of the Greco-Roman world: The idea of sanctification, and of an ultimate cleansing and perfecting of the world and each person, stood in opposition to the Roman view that the past was the best of times, and that things had gotten worse since then.

The Jews, on the other hand, traced their roots back much further, and although some Roman critics did make an effort to "uproot" those roots, others (including the Roman historian Tacitus) accorded the Jews a degree of respect because of the antiquity of their beliefs. In light of this, we can understand efforts by second-century Christian writers to link Christianity to Judaism as much as possible, and thus attain the same antiquity that the Jews were sometimes granted. Critics of Christianity, however, caught on to this tactic and pointed out (however illicitly) that Christians could hardly claim Judaism's antiquity and at the same time observe none of its practices. Therefore, Christianity could never overcome the hurdle of "newness" outside of a limited circle — not without some substantial offering of proof that even though it was a new religion, it had a valid message.

But now compound the problem: Not only was Christianity an arrogant innovator; it was also an *exclusivist* innovator. Many non-Christians today say they are turned off by Christian exclusivity, and the claim that only through Jesus may one be saved (John 14:6). How much more so in the ancient world! How if a faith came telling us we needed to stop attending our churches (and in fact, would prefer that we tear them down!), stop having our parties, and stop observing the social order that had been in place from the time of our venerated ancestors until now? As deSilva notes, "the message about this Christ was incompatible with the most deeply rooted religious ideology of the Gentile world, as well as the more recent message propagated in Roman imperial ideology"[5] (i.e., the *pax Romana*, or enforced peace of Rome, versus the eschatology and judgment of God). The Christians refused to believe in the gods, "the guardians of stability of the world order, the generous patrons who provided all that was needed for sustaining life, as well as the granters of individual petitions." Jews and Christians alike were accused of atheism because they denied the Roman gods. Furthermore, because there was no aspect of social life that was secular — religion in the ancient world was intertwined with public life in a way that would make modern civil liberties attorneys lose their composure — Jews and Christians held themselves aloof from public life, and thereby engendered the indignation of their neighbors who perceived them as standoffish and unconcerned with preserving the social and religious order that was the glue that held the Roman Empire together.

Christianity also seriously undermined deeply-held social convictions. "There is neither Jew nor Greek, there is neither bond nor free, there is neither male nor female: for ye are all one in Christ Jesus," Paul said (Galatians 3:28). You might be so used to applauding this sort of sentiment that you don't realize what a radical message it was for its time and place. In the ancient world, people took their identity from the various groups to which they belonged. Whatever group(s) they were embedded in determined their identity.[6] Changes in persons (such as Paul's conversion) were considered abnormal. Each person had certain role expectations they were expected to fulfill. The erasure or blurring of these various distinctions — stated clearly in Paul, but also done in practice by Jesus during his ministry — would have made Christianity seem radical and offensive to its prospective converts. We may underscore the radical nature of Christianity in its social context by appealing to specific instances of contextually radical behavior by Jesus, the founder of the Christian faith, whose example his disciples followed.

**Forsaking family.** Jesus taught people to break even with family, if needed, for the sake of the Kingdom of God (Matt. 12:49-50), and given the social "deviance" of the Christian movement, a break with one's family was inevitable. Jesus also indicated that his was a highly exclusive religious assembly (Matt. 8:11-12) in a religiously highly inclusive society. Malina and Rohrbaugh note, "Such a departure from the family was something morally impossible in a society where the kinship unit was the focal social institution."[7] The price in this life for the ancients was high — very high indeed — for forsaking family for the Kingdom of God. Leaving the family usually also meant forsaking material goods, in line with Jesus' demand to the rich young ruler (Luke 5:11), but it was the inevitable separation from the family that would have most troubled prospective converts: "Geographical mobility and the consequent break with one's social network (biological family, patrons, friends, neighbors) were considered seriously deviant behavior and would have been much more traumatic in antiquity than simply leaving behind material wealth."[8] How poignant in this light is Peter's confession, "Behold, we have forsaken all, and followed thee; what shall we have therefore?" (Matt. 19:27)

**Reversing Social Roles.** In his teachings, Jesus often featured reversals of common expectations that would have seriously offended his listeners. The "Good Samaritan" parable (Luke 10:30-37) is an example. We all know that Samaritans were despised by the Jews (John 4:9). Making a Samaritan a hero, in a story told to Jews, would have been offensive by itself! The broader context of the story, however, also shows that the *victim* was depicted as someone hated by the everyday Jewish population: The victim (and the Samaritan as well) were traders, who often grew rich at the expense of others, and were despised by the masses who saw them as thieves. Jesus' listeners would actually have sympathized with the bandits who robbed them! Jesus therefore completely reversed the stereotypes of his day in a way that would have shocked his listeners.[9]

Jesus also overturned social expectations in his personal relationships. By dining with the hated tax collector, Zaccheus (Luke 19), Jesus publicly indicated fellowship with one whose values he shared. The crowd was dismayed, because tax collectors were stereotyped as "rapacious extortioners." Zaccheus' pronouncement ("Behold, Lord, the half of my goods I give to the poor; and if I have taken any thing from any man by false accusation, I restore him fourfold."), often understood to mean that he has repented of his former sins and was now paying back what he has stolen, actually means that he *already had been* paying back anyone he discovers he has cheated, even before he met Jesus, and Jesus' fellowship with him is therefore understood as saying to the hostile crowd, "I believe him, and I accept him."[10] Of course, Jesus' association with lepers (Matt. 8:3) and with notorious sinners (Matt. 9:10-11) means that fellowship with Zaccheus was only the tip of the iceberg as far as his questionable associations were concerned!

Here is another example. We may not think much of Mary sitting at Jesus' feet while Martha does the housework (Luke 10:40-2). We may even sympathize with Mary, but the ancients would not have agreed. Because a woman's reputation in the ancient world depended on her ability to run a household, Martha's complaint to Jesus, asking that Mary be sent to help her, would have been seen as legitimate, and Mary herself, because she sat and listened to Jesus teach rather than help with the household chores, was "acting like a male"![11] That Jesus permitted such behavior by a woman would have been shocking to the ancients.

Finally, Jesus' encounter with the Samaritan woman (John 4)[12] — speaking to her in public (both as a woman, and as a social deviant who had been married several times), and using the same drinking utensil — would have offended common Jewish views of purity and group relations. Jesus crossed many deeply-held social and cultural barriers in that single encounter!

**Forsaking Symbols.**[13] As a modern American reacts with offense when someone burns Old Glory, so it is that an ancient Jew would have been offended by things that Jesus did which attacked the recognized symbols of the Jewish worldview, and thereby subverted the unique Jewish ethos that was perceived to have given Israel its identity. Jesus' demonstration in the Temple (Matt. 21:12-13) was a symbolic "acting out" of the destruction of what, to many Jews, was Judaism's central symbol: the place where sacrifice and forgiveness of sins was effected; a place of great prestige and honor before non-Jews, and the central political symbol of Israel. Not all Jews agreed with this assessment (for example, the Essenes, the authors of the Dead Sea Scrolls, considered the Temple apparatus corrupt and probably would have sympathized with Jesus on this point), but for Jesus to say the Temple would be destroyed, and by pagans at that (Luke 21:20), would have been profoundly offensive to nearly all Jews, especially those who considered the Temple to be security against pagan invasion.

**Teaching Subversion.** As if the Temple demonstration were not bad enough, Jesus' teachings also undermined the Jewish perception of patriotism. The general attitude towards pagan powers like Rome was revolution. Jesus advised instead "turning the other cheek" and carrying the soldier's pack an extra mile (Matt. 5:41). The difference is one of Malcolm X versus Martin Luther King, in a time when Malcolm X's methods were more highly favored.

Jesus also undercut Jewish perceptions of the law in several instances. Jesus' actions of healing (Mark 3), and plucking corn (Matthew 12), on the Sabbath of course did not violate the actual law, but the rigorous interpretation of the law favored by those wishing to preserve and emphasize the distinction the law gave them. Jesus' giving his disciples permission to dispense with ritual hand-washing (Matt. 15:2 — like the "stickler" Sabbath observance, not a rule of the law, but a rigorous interpretation of it) violated common perceptions of purity. Finally, Jesus' command to follow him, rather than bury the dead (Matt. 8:22), violated one of the most ingrained sensibilities of the day to care for the family and attend to their burial needs (important both in Jewish and non-Jewish contexts).

So it is that Christianity turned the norms of the ancient world upside down, and said that birth, ethnicity, gender, and wealth — those factors which determined a person's honor and worth in this social setting — meant nothing. There was little reason why an ancient person would have found such a movement desirable to join. "But," you may ask, "what about slaves and members of the lower class? Surely they would have welcomed the chance to be treated as equals." So we may think at first, but the objection falsely imposes our modern sense of egalitarianism upon people who had no such sense of social order. For the ancients, it would have been out of order to not stand in some sort of dependent relationship. "When ancient Mediterraneans speak of 'freedom,' they generally understand the term as both freedom from slavery to one lord or master, and freedom to enter the service of another lord or benefactor."[14] It would also not have occurred to such persons as a whole that their situation could be changed so readily, since all that happened was attributed to fate, fortune, or providence.[15] As an ancient, you did not fight your situation; you endured it, and to endure your lot was the most honorable thing to do — unless something unusual (like the Resurrection!) gave you a way out. Life was not a matter of whether you were in service to another, but who you were in service to.

The social factor of group identity therefore marks another proof of Christianity's authenticity. In a group-oriented society like the ancient Mediterranean, a person received their identity from their group leader, and people needed the endorsement of others to support their identity. Christianity forced a severing of social and religious ties, the things which made an ancient person "human" in standing. As Malina and Rohrbaugh note:

> *Given the sharp social stratification prevalent in antiquity, persons engaging in inappropriate social relations risked being cut off from networks on which their positions depended. In traditional societies this was taken with deadly seriousness. Alienation from family or clan could literally be a matter of life and death, especially for the elite, who would risk everything by the wrong kind of association with the wrong kind of people. Since the inclusive Christian communities demanded just this kind of association across kinship status lines, the situation depicted [in Matt. 10:34-36] is realistic indeed. The alienation would even spread beyond the family of origin to the larger kinship network formed by marriage...*[16]

"Association" included being seen eating with persons of lower social rank. The practice of partaking of the Lord's Supper with people below your class would have been by itself a social *faux pas* of the highest order! Christianity, of course, did provide community support of its own in return, but that hardly explains why people joined the movement in the first place. Given the social pressures ancient Christians would have been under, ranging from social ostracization to loss of property to even martyrdom, it is extremely unlikely that anyone would have accepted the Christian faith — unless it had indisputable evidence of its central claim, the Resurrection of Jesus Christ.

## Notes

[1] Robert Wilken, *The Christians as the Romans Saw Them* (Yale University Press, 1986), 62.

[2] Ibid., 63.

[3] Malina and Neyrey, *Portraits of Paul,* 164.

[4] John J. Pilch and Bruce J. Malina, *Handbook of Biblical Social Values* (Peabody, MA: Hendrickson, 1988), 19.

[5] deSilva, *Honor,* 46.

[6] This "group identity" factor also makes it unlikely that Jesus could have kept a ministry going unless those around him supported him and his Messianic identity claims. A merely human Jesus could not have met this demand and must have provided convincing proofs of his power and authority to maintain a following, and for a movement to have started and survived well beyond him. Such a Jesus would have had to live up to the expectations of others, and would have been abandoned, or at least had to change his methods, at the first significant sign of failure.

[7] Bruce J. Malina and Richard L. Rohrbaugh, *Social-Science Commentary on the Synoptic Gospels* (Minneapolis: Fortress Press, 1992), 244.

[8] Ibid., 313.

[9] Ibid., 347.

[10] Ibid., 387.

[11] Ibid., 348.

[12] Bruce J. Malina and Richard L. Rohrbaugh, *Social-Science Commentary on the Gospel of John* (Minneapolis: Fortress Press, 1998), 98-9.

[13] Ideas from this section are derived from N. T. Wright's *Jesus and the Victory of God* (Minneapolis: Fortress Press, 1997), 369-442.

[14] Malina and Neyrey, *Portraits of* Paul, 163.

[15] Ibid., 189.

[16] Malina and Rohrbaugh, *Social-Science Commentary on the Synoptic Gospels*, 92.

# *"But What About...?"*

*Isaiah 46:9 Remember the former things of old: for I am God, and there is none else; I am God, and there is none like me...*

An obvious response for a skeptic to make to our arguments so far is, "So what? The same could be said of other religions. Christianity isn't special." A person should certainly be challenged to prove such a response with specifics. It is not enough to simply say that the same factors could apply to any or all religions, as though by mere statement this were the case.

Obviously it would be impossible to examine here each and every religious tradition in the world and throughout history, to see if any pass the test of an "impossible faith." But it is possible to examine some leading competitors, and suggest by their example that no other successful religious faith, past or present, has had as many challenges to overcome as Christianity did, and to show that they had or now have advantages which Christianity did not enjoy. For comparison, let's analyze the history behind three leading challengers: *Mithraism*, Christianity's leading religious competitor in the ancient world; *Mormonism*, today's fastest-growing religion; and *Islam*, the largest monotheistic world religion other than Christianity. Concerning each of these three faiths, we will begin with some preliminary information, and then ask three questions:

*First,* did the leading personage or figure in this faith do or say anything that would have been considered dishonorable or disreputable, and if so, would that have affected the movement as a whole, as the Crucifixion affected Christianity?

*Second,* were there any social prejudices that the movement would have had to deal with, as Christianity would have had to deal with Jesus being a Jew from Nazareth in Galilee?

*Third,* did the movement offer any teachings that were contrary to deeply-held convictions within its social setting, such as Christianity's belief in resurrection and its radical restructuring of the social order?

**Candidate One: Mithraism**

If you've never heard of the ancient pagan deity Mithra, you're not alone. The cult of Mithra died out in the fourth century, and there are only a handful of scholars today who specialize in its study.[1] Mithraism was an ancient "mystery religion" that celebrated the slaying of a cosmic bull (represented by the constellation of Taurus) by the deity Mithra. The Mithraic movement left behind no scriptures, and very little documentary evidence about itself. However, it is generally recognized that Mithraists underwent ritual initiations that they believed gave them a form of eternal life as exalted spirits.

*Did the leading personage or figure in this faith do or say anything that would have been considered dishonorable or disreputable?* There is nothing associated with Mithra to suggest that he would have been associated with shame or ignominy. His slaying of the cosmic bull was looked upon as heroic and useful. Mithra showed no apparent weaknesses, did exactly what the ancients would have expected a deity to be able to do, and acted the way a deity was supposed to act.

*Were there any social prejudices that the movement would have had to deal with?* Mithra was a divine being, not a human, so ethnic prejudices would not apply. He was a god with a Persian background, and the people of the east were enemies of the Romans. However, this disadvantage is countered by a Roman fascination with mysterious oriental ideas which would not benefit Christianity, preaching its tangible human from Galilee.

*Did the movement offer any teachings that were contrary to deeply-held convictions within its social setting?* Based on what testimony we have from ancient writers who described Mithraic beliefs, the answer is *no*. Mithraism did not teach objectionable doctrines and was not exclusivist. It did, however, remain a socially exclusive faith, excluding women from its ranks in line with the social mores of the day.

The one disadvantage Mithraism may have had was that it was, in a sense, a newer religion. Mithraic scholars connect the origin of Roman Mithraism to the passage of the precession of the equinoxes in 128 B. C., when it was discovered that the celestial equinox had recently passed through Taurus (the "bull" slain by Mithra). However, whatever newness the Mithraic faith may have had was substantially offset in effect by its connection to Mithra as a Persian god with a much longer history (dating back to at least 1400 B. C.) and by the tying of the movement's origin to a mighty stellar phenomenon like the precession of the equinoxes.[2] Mithraism may have even appealed to the historical occurrence of the precession as justification for antiquity.

Finally, Mithraism had two advantages that Christianity did not. The first advantage was the appeal of oriental mysticism to the Romans, and Mithraism's similarities to other ancient mystery rites of the day. The second advantage is more imposing: Mithraism was particularly popular among members of the Roman military. Even if the movement had taught unusual or unpopular beliefs, it is unlikely that anyone outside the movement would have objected when members of the movement could arrange for an arrest or an untimely death. Mithraism had an advantage of members with power. Clearly, it comes nowhere near the classification of an "impossible faith."

## Candidate Two: Mormonism

What better candidate for comparison to the "impossible faith" of Christianity than its derivative faith, Mormonism? Mormonism is today's fastest-growing religion, currently with over 11 million members, and a rate of growth that will give it a membership as large as 250 million by the year 2050.[3] So how does this strongly missionary faith fare when compared to historic Christianity?

*Did the leading personage or figure in this faith do or say anything that would have been considered dishonorable or disreputable?* The answer to this question is *yes* — but requires a significant set of caveats. As noted in Chapter 1, the matter is not merely that that Jesus was subjected to a dishonorable and ignominious death, and to other instances of dishonor, but that he was subjected to these things in a society where *honor was deeply valued.* Mormonism emerged in American society. We do not entirely dispense with honor, but it is by far a secondary or tertiary concern. If we do not already despise an individual, we naturally sympathize with them when they are suffering, and if a man is unjustly executed, our sympathy increases many-fold. Ours is a society with a deep focus upon the individual.

What, then, of shame and dishonor in Mormonism? The office of Joseph Smith as Prophet is roughly comparable to Jesus' headship of the church in terms of this discussion. Smith did endure a number of dishonorable experiences: He was tarred and feathered, jailed, beaten up, and reviled. However, such treatment does not mean the same thing in a society where honor is not a primary value, or where the individual is valued over the collective. Smith had many enemies, but he also had many friends and allies who, even as they disagreed with his views, nevertheless gave him aid. Moreover, the core of belief in what Smith preached was not integral to any dishonorable experience or act as it was with Christianity. Christianity was staked in the Crucifixion and had to preach it. Mormonism has no stake in Smith's sufferings in the same way and could technically not mention them.

In sum, while Smith was subjected to dishonor on several occasions, his experience is moot in this context, because it did not mean the same thing in his day as it would have in the ancient Mediterranean. If anything, because of the nature of the dishonor (inflicted as it was most often by others), the treatment he underwent also drew him more friends.

*Were there any social prejudices that the movement would have had to deal with?* There were social prejudices in America of the 19th century, but Smith was not affected by the most serious: The racial factor. Smith's roots in the state of New York as a poor and rural agriculturalist would perhaps have been a negative signal to residents of urban areas, and to those in the South. However, the historical record shows that Mormonism did not have to engage in this conflict to any serious extent. Indeed, those who were more like Smith than not were in the far majority. Mormonism also existed in a national (and to some extent international) hegemony unlike the Roman Empire with its various nations and prejudices.

*Did the movement offer any teachings that were contrary to deeply-held convictions within its social setting?* The answer is *yes* — but with stronger caveats. Mormonism offers an example of a faith that had to move and change to survive. Most of the doctrines of Mormonism are, or have been, either in line with already accepted Christian doctrine (incarnation, convert baptism, resurrection), or are unusual, but generally non-offensive (baptism for the dead, pre-existence of the soul). At least two historic practices of Mormonism, however, were considered to be as repulsive as resurrection would have been to the pagans and Romans: polygamy, and the historic Mormon understanding of the inferiority of non-Caucasian races. Both of these were practices which Mormonism eventually gave up — the former under intense military and political pressure, the latter under tremendous social pressure.[4] In this regard, Mormonism parallels the social path of the Sabbatean movement rather than historic Christianity.

Admittedly, Mormons did suffer a tremendous amount of social pressure, and yet remained faithful to their beliefs. Joseph Smith was Mormonism's martyr *par excellence*, but far from the only one, and persecution was inflicted upon the Saints in every place they ventured. Mormons were shot at, killed, beaten, and hounded from place to place. Officials called for their removal or extermination. Armies pursued them even to Utah. Their homes were burned and their innocents murdered. This is overall a black spot on our history and cannot be downplayed.

However, the Mormons had some advantages that the early Christians did not. While some persecuted the Mormons, others were sympathetic and offered the Mormons temporary shelter and respite. This would not have been the case for the early Christians. Mormonism also grew in a frontier society where there was ample land for expansion, and places to remove entire communities and easily heed the advice, "when they persecute you in one town, flee to another." One may justly ask whether Mormonism today would be the same institution had it not had Nauvoo, Illinois, and later Utah, to flee to, and to regroup in — and then, had it not eventually compromised (for whatever reason is claimed) on its most socially offensive doctrine (polygamy) in that early period. Early Christians, in contrast, had no place to flee other than wilderness and the perhaps catacombs, and could not count on any sympathetic allies. Would Mormonism have survived the tyranny and the injustice of the Roman Empire?

Yet what of Mormons not giving up their core beliefs in spite of persecution? Critics may retort that "in every religion, people die for their beliefs." This is true. However, in most cases the beliefs in question are not grounded in historical data, and are much easier to still believe in and die for than a faith held in a fact of history like the Resurrection. One who would readily die for the belief that there were three or five gods, or that the dead received salvation, or that one will receive a certain eternal reward, may not be so ready to die for a belief that Washington did (or did not) cross the Delaware, or that Nero fiddled (or did not) while Rome burned, or that Kennedy was elected (or not elected) President. With all of Mormonism's historical claims either inaccessible for most of its history (Book of Mormon events)[5] or rooted in private events (revelations to Smith and others), and with all of its theological claims (other than those borrowed from Christianity) not rooted in history otherwise, Mormonism was more like the former on this account than the latter.[6]

Perhaps Mormonism's greatest theological risk was its claim that the vast majority of the present Christian church was apostate, and that Smith's revelations provided the key to a "restoration." This was a bold claim indeed, but it also resonated well, in part because to an obvious extent, to the average person, it seemed to be true! Just as today, many of the churches in Smith's time preached messages that seemed, to the average person, to be confused, difficult, contradictory, and questionable. Mormonism offered a simplified fine-tuning that was not entirely innovative, merely innovative on certain points that made the message easier to digest. It also did not upset the social order, as it accepted overall the same moral values (outside of polygamy) as the rest of the society around it. There is no parallel to the Roman conception that failing to pay homage to the proper gods (piety) would cause problems in other arenas, and given freedom of religious faith in America, no conflict with the political ideology. Beyond that, as an individualistic society, America had (and still has) a "live and let live" approach that would have been foreign to the ancients. Once Mormonism dropped polygamy, they were free to live in peace in spite of any other unusual doctrines or practices that were otherwise lawful.

In conclusion, Mormonism simply does not pass the test of an "impossible faith." Despite some difficulties it encountered, the fact that it compromised on offensive doctrines, and that it emerged in a society that offered it just as many sympathizers as enemies, means that it is a very much "possible" faith that has followed the social course we would expect from any otherwise unremarkable religious movement.

**Candidate Three: Islam**

The last of our three candidates, the world religion of Islam, offers the most complex history. Islam began in a political situation in which two large empires — the Byzantines and the Sasanians — competed for supremacy. These two empires were centrally at odds, politically, philosophically (Hellenist vs. Iranian/Semitic), and religiously (Christian vs. Zoroastrian). Beside the two empires were a few independent territories, including Axum in Arabia, where Muhammed was born. Arabia at the time of Muhammed's birth was a land rent with strife, "in the grip of a chronic cycle of warfare and violence" exacerbated by a tribal system which perpetuated disunity.[7] Islam emerged in difficult and trying historical circumstances, and could rightly be described as impressive faith, even an incredible faith — but does it pass the test of an "impossible faith"?

*Did the leading personage or figure in this faith do or say anything that would have been considered dishonorable or disreputable?* The general answer to this question is *no*. There was obviously no trial or crucifixion to speak of, and Muhammed did not have a disreputable or questionable background. He had been orphaned, but came under the guardianship of his prestigious uncles, and was a member of an Arabian tribe that had a "measure of experience in the organization and management of people and materials." Early accounts show Muhammed to have been "a promising and respected young man who participated in both Mecca's cultic activities and commerce."[8] He earned the nickname "al-Amin," or "the reliable one" because of his "ability to inspire confidence in others."[9] Stories of Muhammed show him to have been known as a judicious and shrewd manager of people.[10]

Muhammed was not completely free of controversy during his lifetime. The prophet of Islam took several risks. At one time he permitted the raiding of a caravan during a sacred month when the feuding Arab tribes would cease hostilities. (He did, however, react immediately to protests by repudiating the raid and refusing to accept any of the captured booty.)[11] He married his adopted son's ex-wife, as commanded by a revelation, in spite of some critics who thought the match would be incestuous.[12] Perhaps the most risky behavior he engaged was forging a treaty with the pagans (the treaty of Hudaybiyya) which included terms that were extremely humiliating for his followers. The shock of this compromise was so great that even one of Muhammad's staunchest and most loyal followers, Umar, wanted to secede from the community. However, Muhammed gave his followers an immediate assurance that Allah was "mysteriously present" in the seeming defeat, and true to his abilities, Muhammed quickly out-calculated his opponents, taking advantage of loopholes in the treaty and turnings its restrictions to his own advantage.[13]

*Were there any social prejudices that the movement would have had to deal with?* Islam began within the relatively limited confines of Arabia among persons of common ancestry. No one thought less of Muhammed because he was from Mecca or because of his genealogy. Indeed, Muhammed's ancestry helped him in the long run. He belonged to a tribe called the Quraysh, which had tremendous prestige in Arabia as guardians of the most ancient temple of the Arabs in their hometown of Mecca, and they possessed greater wealth and security than any other tribe in Arabia.[14] Other tribes believed that the Quraysh were divinely favored because around the time of Muhammad's birth, a large Abyssinian Christian army had set out from the south to destroy the Meccan temple. They made it to Mecca, but the mission was aborted, for mysterious reasons. Muslims believe that it was because God sent a large flight of birds to pelt the invading army with "poisonous pebbles," while naturalistic historians think there was an outbreak of smallpox in the Abyssinian army. This stunning turn of events made the Quraysh appear to be divinely favored in the sight of the Arabs, because it seemed that God had mysteriously defended them from the invading army.[15] Thus, when Muhammad himself later decisively marched on Mecca, and overwhelmed the Quraysh without any bloodshed or fighting, the Arabs began to think of him as divinely protected and favored. From that point on, delegations poured in from all over the Arabian peninsula acknowledging him as God's apostle.

*Did the movement offer any teachings that were contrary to deeply-held convictions within its social setting?* The answer is *yes* – but as with Mormonism, there are substantial caveats to offer.

Esposito notes that in some ways, what Muhammed had to offer was neither new nor unusual. "Many aspects of Muhammed's message were conveyed in concepts and sometimes words that were already familiar in Arabia...The ideas of monotheism, a Last Judgment, heaven and hell, prophecy and revelations, and the emphasis on intense, even militant, piety were widespread in the Near Eastern scripturalist religions in the sixth century."[16] The Qu'ran did not necessarily reveal anything unknown to the Arabians, as much as it encouraged them to act on and be consistent with things they already knew.[17] Yet Muhammed's origins with the Quraysh, and the general religious climate of Arabia, guaranteed that his message would fight an uphill battle for reception. The Quraysh and many Arabian tribes still believed in pagan religions which they were reluctant to abandon in favor of monotheism,[18] and some of Muhammed's most fierce opposition came from within his own tribe. Muhammed did have to fight an attitude somewhat like the Roman one: "We will follow the religion our forefathers followed." Given the tight nature of familial relations in ancient Arabia, Muhammed's religious message "set a man at variance against his father, and the daughter against her mother, and the daughter in law against her mother in law." At times this required men to fight sword to sword with those in their own families who did not convert from paganism. Muhammed's lack of compromise on this central issue was a significant risk.[19]

Islamic doctrines and practices caused no small amount of controversy as well. Islam teaches resurrection, and while the movement did not come up against Greco-Roman aversions to the material body, it did have to overcome a less sophisticated form of this objection from pagans who could not imagine someone living again after becoming dust and bones, and did not believe in an afterlife.[20] Muhammed's teaching of a final judgment also offended the sensibilities of the wealthier members of his tribe who did not appreciate the idea that their wealth and power would be of no help to them.[21]

Early in his prophetic career, Muhammed found himself in desperate straits. The members of his tribe desired to kill him for insulting their religion and mocking their way of life. Only the protection of Muhammed's prestigious uncle, Abu Talib, kept him safe.[22] His converts began to be persecuted and insulted, leading Muhammed to find them sanctuary away from Mecca, in Abyssinia. This persecution, however, was clearly not as serious as that experienced by early Christians, being "mainly confined to trade sanctions and verbal abuse once the most vulnerable Muslims had gone to Abyssinia."[23] At a later date, hostile members of the Quraysh organized a treaty among the non-Muslim clans agreeing to subject Muhammed's followers to an economic and social boycott, but this lasted only two years before the Arab sensitivity for family got the better of the oppressors who could not bear to see their Muslim relatives in desperate straits, and even before the boycott ended some were sending the Muslims food and supplies surreptitiously.[24]

Islam's story is an amazing and even incredible one, and it might even meet the test of an "impossible faith" — except for one factor: Muhammed's road to success via political leadership, and when necessary, the sword. Muslims may argue, quite sensibly from their perspective, that Allah gifted Muhammed with victories and with military and social genius. Indeed, one particular Islamic website explains:

> *We find, on this occasion, the Prophet exhibiting the marvelous qualities of an experienced military tactician, which complemented his eternal mission of delivering the universal guidance to mankind, providing yet another indication that the inspiration received by him could have only been from Almighty God. The way in which he organized his troops for battle, as well as his reactions to the sudden and surprise attacks by the superior enemy forces despite the limited number of soldiers needs to be studied to truly appreciate the prodigious military genius of the Prophet.*[25]

The historical record shows that Muhammed was indeed a careful and brilliant tactician, both militarily and socially. Muhammed grew his movement slowly, at first gaining enough converts to take over a single city, Yathrib (now Medina), and then gradually expanding his influence. He spent ten years consolidating his control, in the process dealing with those who challenged his prophetic authority (or allied themselves with his political enemies). His opponents "were handled harshly in a series of confrontations" and exiled, enslaved, or executed.[26] Once control of Medina was secure, Muhammed orchestrated raids on camel caravans, the "commercial lifeblood" of Mecca, until they finally negotiated a truce. Later, when Muhammed assumed control of Mecca itself, he won the loyalty of members of his old tribe by giving them positions of authority. From there he eventually became "the most powerful political leader in Arabia."[27]

After Muhammed's death, his successors continued a military-oriented policy. His immediate successor, Abu Bakr, reacted to attempts to abandon the political and religious alliances "quickly and decisively in what is usually called the Apostasy (or Ridda) wars, during which he sent armed bands of Believers to the main centers of opposition in Arabia."[28] It was not long before the movement controlled all of the Arabian peninsula, and started biting chunks off of the Byzantines and Sasanins, the latter of whom they managed to defeat completely. As a whole, though, they were not harsh taskmasters to the newly conquered peoples, forcing only pagans (and sometimes Zoroastrians) to convert to the new faith while leaving Jews and Christians alone. They also implemented an efficient system of "highly clustered garrison settlements" that became new cities, which in turn helped the Muslims live apart from the subject peoples of their vast conquests, thereby minimizing assimilation with them.

One cannot help but note that the tactical brilliance of Muhammed and his successors serves to show just how impossible Christianity was in its own context, for it had no such advantages. There was no political or military genius at the helm of the Christian faith, and theological geniuses like Paul had no hardware to back themselves up. Islam, unlike Christianity, did not spend very long as an underdog, and never was an underdog to a huge Empire that despised what it stood for. Had Muhammed not been such a brilliant tactician, what would Islam be today?

In light of the above, we must conclude that Islam does not pass the test as an "impossible faith." Muhammed was clearly an amazing individual, like the CEO of today who gambled and won big. But one may reasonably ask whether Islam would have succeeded had his gambles come to nought.

## Notes

[1] An excellent general introduction to Mithraism is David Ulansey's *The Origins of the Mithraic Mysteries: Cosmology and Salvation in the Ancient World* (New York: Oxford University Press, 1989).

[2] Ulansey suggests that the origin of Mithraism rested in Stoic intellectuals in Tarsus who saw a divine being behind every natural

force such as the precession: "...[I]t would not be surprising if our group of Stoics hypothesized the existence of a new divine being which was responsible for this previously unknown motion of the cosmic structure." *Mithraic Mysteries,* 82.

[3] Richard N. Ostling and Joan K. Ostling, *Mormon America: The Power and the Promise* (San Francisco: HarperSanFrancisco, 1999), 372, 375.

[4] Interestingly, among Mormonism's original defenses of the polygamy doctrine was one typically American: "Whose business is it? Hands off here! Our belief is our own! We have a right to our opinion!" — a "defense" which would have never worked in the ancient world, in a collectivist society where everyone minded everyone else's business (see chapters 9 and 10)! Coke Newell, *Latter Days: Six Billion Years of Mormonism* (New York: St. Martin's, 2000), 108.

[5] Mormonism maintains a belief in an alternate course of history in the Western Hemisphere, involving the transplantation of exploring Jews from Palestine to Central America, and their establishment of a kingdom here. Christian apologists have made much of the lack of hard evidence for this alternate history. However, this controversy has taken place primarily in our century. At the time of Joseph Smith, the testing of such claims was almost completely impossible, and the events described in the Book of Mormon were separated by time and distance from prospective Mormon converts.

Mormon apologists are busily seeking verification for this history. In the meantime, the faithful await, mostly not concerned, in a society that has accepted the premise that faith doesn't need history to support it, and "what's true for you may not be true for me." Nevertheless, it is worth asking whether Mormonism will have to change to survive as their alternate history of the Americas is subjected to more research and scrutiny.

[6] One exception may be argued: The witnesses to the gold plates which Smith allegedly unearthed, and used to create the Book of Mormon. Smith of course may have possessed some item or items which were purportedly gold plates. What they

were, or if any such item existed, is a matter beyond our scope. However, possession of such items is far less significant in scope than claiming observation of, and extended interchange with, a resurrected man.

[7] Karen Armstrong, *Muhammed: A Biography of the Prophet* (San Francisco: HarperSanFrancisco, 1992), 65.

[8] John Esposito, *The Oxford History of Islam* (Oxford: Oxford University Press, 1999), 6.

[9] Armstrong, *Muhammed,* 78.

[10] Armstrong, 81-2, recounts the example of Muhammed resolving conflict between members of Quraysh clans who each wanted the honor of placing the final, sacred stone at the conclusion of a refurbishing of the Meccan temple. Muhammed had the men bring a cloak and place the final stone in the center of it, then instructed each clan to have one member take hold of the edge of the cloak, and lift the stone into its place together!

[11] Ibid., 171.

[12] Ibid., 196.

[13] Ibid., 222-8.

[14] Ibid., 45.

[15] Ibid., 67. Armstrong recounts the words said of the Quraysh: "They are the people of God; God fought for them and thwarted the attack of their enemies."

[16] Ibid., 7-8.

[17] Ibid., 95.

[18] Ibid., 52-3, 107. Indeed, Armstrong notes that when Muhammed first pressed the issue of monotheism, he "lost most of his supporters overnight."

[19] Ibid., 108. We leave aside here the matter of the so-called "Satanic verses" in which Muhammed allegedly made a concession to polytheism by allowing certain pagan goddesses to be admitted as intermediaries. Many Muslims regard this story

as apocryphal. However, even if it is true, Muhammed almost immediately rejected any polytheistic implications, and at other, later times clearly refused to compromise on this doctrine.

[20] Ibid., 59, 106-7

[21] Ibid., 106-7.

[22] Ibid., 119.

[23] Ibid., 122-4.

[24] Ibid., 129, 132

[25] Found at <http://www.islamvision.org/badr.htm>.

[26] Esposito, *Oxford History of Islam*, 8.

[27] Ibid., 10.

[28] Ibid., 11.

# *The Three Pillars of Early Evangelism*

*Acts 2:22-25 Ye men of Israel, hear these words; Jesus of Nazareth, a man approved of God among you by miracles and wonders and signs, which God did by him in the midst of you, as ye yourselves also know: Him, being delivered by the determinate counsel and foreknowledge of God, ye have taken, and by wicked hands have crucified and slain: Whom God hath raised up, having loosed the pains of death: because it was not possible that he should be holden of it. For David speaketh concerning him, I foresaw the Lord always before my face, for he is on my right hand, that I should not be moved...*

*Acts 26:26 For the king knoweth of these things, before whom also I speak freely: for I am persuaded that none of these things are hidden from him; for this thing was not done in a corner.*

Following Pentecost, how would the disciples of Jesus have spread word of the Resurrection? What evidence and arguments would they have presented for the divinity of Jesus and for the Resurrection? Modern courses in evangelism stress the technique of offering one's *personal testimony*, and given this emphasis you may assume that the technique is explicitly mandated, in the Bible. But it isn't.

The closest any New Testament writer gets to offering a personal testimony is Philippians 3, where Paul tells his readers how his life was changed by Jesus. He explicitly refers to his former life as a zealous Pharisee, willing to persecute Christians unto death, and says of this former life, "...I count all things but loss for the excellency of the knowledge of Christ Jesus my Lord: for whom I have suffered the loss of all things, and do count them but dung, that I may win Christ" (Phil. 3:8). While this sounds like a personal testimony, it is actually part of a letter to *fellow Christians* in which Paul contrasts himself to "evil workers" (Phil. 3:2) who opposed him. Paul was not witnessing of his faith as an evangelist, but was setting a contrast for vulnerable believers between himself and those who were preaching false doctrine and were motivated by pride. No such personal testimony is ever delivered evangelistically to non-believers.

As the quote from Acts at the beginning of this chapter shows, early missionary preaching mainly appealed to *facts* about Jesus. Peter, Paul, and others called for repentance on three grounds, which we will call the "pillars of early evangelism," that constituted the Christian Gospel message:

**Appeal #1: Miracles, wonders, and signs.** Peter explicitly refers to Jesus as "a man approved of God among you by miracles and wonders and signs." The many public miracles of Jesus — the man whose withered hand he restored (Matt. 12:10), the lepers he cleansed (Luke 17:11-14), even the wine he miraculously produced at Cana (John 2:1-10) — would have provided substantive testimony to his divine authority. Thereafter, and throughout Acts, the public miracles experienced and performed by the Apostles — the tongues falling at Pentecost (Acts 2:3-11), the healing of the man who sat at the Temple gate (Acts 3:1-11), Paul's public exorcism of a familiar spirit (Acts 16:18) — would have similarly provided authority for the Gospel message they preached. The Apostles also undoubtedly appealed to the darkness at the time of the Crucifixion (Matthew 27:45, Mark 15:33, Luke 23:44) and the signs within the Temple (Matthew 27:51, Mark 15:38, Luke 23:45) as evidence of God's vindication of Jesus.

**Appeal #2: The Empty Tomb.** The Resurrection of Jesus was the central fact of the Christian Gospel, and it is appealed to time and time again in the church's missionary preaching (Acts 2:24, 32; 3:15; 4:10; 5:30; 10:40; 13:30; 17:31).

**Appeal #3: The fulfillment of Old Testament prophecy by Jesus.** Throughout the Gospels and in Acts, the New Testament claims that Jesus specifically fulfilled Old Testament prophecy in his historical actions.[1] Peter in Acts 2:17-20 claims that the falling of the tongues on the believers was a fulfillment of Joel 2:28-32. In Acts 2:25-36 he claims that Jesus fulfilled Psalms 16:8-11 and 110:1. Matthew 2:15 claims that Jesus fulfilled Hosea 11:1, and Matthew 4:14-16 claims that Jesus fulfilled Isaiah 9:1-2.

These three appeals, although varied in their subject matter, all return to the same basic premise: God *acted in history* in a public way, and these public displays testified to the historical reality upon which the Christian faith was grounded. They were things that could be checked out and confirmed by those who listened to the Gospel message. People could see that a man lame from birth (Acts 3:1ff), or blind from birth (John 9:1ff) had been healed; local persons could testify to the former status of the healed person. They knew (or could find out) that the Temple curtain had been torn, and that darkness had been over the land, precisely at the time Jesus had been crucified. They could see for themselves the Apostles performing signs and wonders. They could ask whether Jesus had indeed gone to Egypt as a child. None of these things, as Paul said to Agrippa, had been done in a corner.

A skeptic may object, however, that it is unrealistic to expect people to have cared enough about

Christian claims to check into them, and even if they did care enough, to have expected them to take the time or have the ability to check them out. What would a peasant in Rome care if a man came saying that an obscure Jewish preacher had been raised in Palestine? And if he did care, how would he be able to get to Palestine and talk to the right people? The skeptic will simply answer that Christianity simply found enough gullible people to accept its message, and that was how it grew. Case closed.

We would agree that the bulk of people approached by missionaries would simply dismiss their claims without further consideration. But beyond the threshold of the social factors we have explored, gullibility will not serve as an adequate explanation for Christian success that *did* occur among hundreds of thousands of people all over the Empire. This is merely an easy excuse that does not explain how this supposed gullibility caused these early Christians to ignore firmly-cherished values and customs that were polar opposites from those that Christianity offered. The smug appeal to "gullibility" is little more than an exercise in avoiding a more detailed reply that actually confronts the data. It is a begged question that simply says, "Well, they must have been stupid enough to believe in spite of all of that, because otherwise, we would not be here!" This is an unacceptable response, not only because it is too simple, but also for two quite substantial reasons that shatter the premise that Christianity was merely believed in by gullible people.

Here is the first reason. We as Americans value our privacy; this orientation would make life very hard on us in the Biblical world. The ancient Mediterranean was a society of a sort that anthropologists call "group-oriented". In such societies, behavioral codes are enforced by the group, and the people continually mind each other's business. Neighbors exerted "constant vigilance" over others; those they watched were constantly concerned for appearances, and the associated rewards of honor or sanctions of shame that came with the results.[2] In such a society, strangers, such as the early Christian missionaries would have been, were viewed as posing a threat to the community, because "they are potentially anything one cares to imagine...Hence, they must be checked over both as to how they might fit in and as to whether they will subscribe to the community's norms."[3] Missionaries would find their virtues tested at every new stopping point.

Ancient people controlled one another's behavior by watching their neighbors, and by spreading word of deviant behavior. In a society where nothing escaped notice, there was indeed every reason to suppose that people hearing the Gospel message would check against the facts — especially where a movement with a radical message like Christianity was concerned. Thus, the empty tomb story *would* be checked. Matthew's story of resurrected saints would be tested for witnesses and confirmation. Lazarus would be sought out for questioning. Excessive honor claims, such as that Jesus had been vindicated, or his claims to be divine, would have been given close scrutiny. Checking of the facts would be inevitable, since it would be assumed that checking Christian claims, and presumably disproving them, would help control the deviant Christian movement. Think of it this way: If the Pharisees checked Jesus on things like handwashing and grain picking; if large crowds gathered around Jesus each time he so much as opened his mouth, how much more would things like a claimed resurrection have been examined! Gullibility, for this reason alone, is not a sufficient answer.

There is a second response, however, that is even more damaging to the appeal to gullibility. An analysis of the converts who are mentioned in the New Testament shows that early Christianity was top-heavy in terms of those who had higher social status. In the Greco-Roman world, an extreme majority of the people were poor or living in wretched conditions, but for its size, Christianity had an unusual number of the rich and the powerful in its ranks. As the Biblical scholar E. A. Judge has put it:

> *...the Christians were dominated by a socially pretentious section of the population of big cities. Beyond that they seem to have drawn on a broad constituency, probably representing the household dependents of leading members.* [4]

Christianity therefore had among its membership people who would be the most educated, and the least likely to be gullible, and the most likely to be concerned with the social factors we have laid out in previous chapters. They would be the persons who had the most to lose, and the least to gain, in terms of worldly interests, by becoming converts to this new and strange religion.

With that, a final objection may now be dealt with. A critic may ask, "Well, how could these people have evaluated the claims of these early missionaries? They couldn't get on the Internet and look things up." No, they could not. But it was precisely this socially pretentious section of Greco-Roman society that had the time and the resources needed to travel, or to send travelers, to do the needed investigative work, to send letters, to ask questions of the right officials, and report their findings to others. Moreover, many of the acts of Jesus and the Apostles were witnessed by Jews from all over the Roman Empire, who returned to Jerusalem for the Jewish festivals on a regular basis, giving them ample opportunity to seek out and question persons who would have the needed knowledge.[5] It is our contention that many of Christianity's first converts beyond Jerusalem (where the facts were already easily accessible) were people who originally set out to disprove the faith's claims, as a means of trying to get the new and strange movement under control, and ended up being stymied by the ultimate rebuttal — a certain, trustworthy, and undeniable witness to the life, miracles, and finally, the resurrection of Jesus, the only event which, in the eyes of the ancients, would have vindicated Jesus' honor and overcome the innumerable stigma of his life and death. It was an event that had certainty that could not be denied, having enough early witnesses (such as the 500 witnesses mentioned by Paul), and having enough solid and indisputable testimony that made it harder to not believe than to believe.

## Notes

[1] A separate but related issue often brought up in this context is the alleged liberties taken by the New Testament authors with the Old Testament text. Such arguments may be refuted by showing parallels between the New Testament exegetical models and other ancient Jewish methods of exegesis, which demonstrate that the New Testament writers did not use the Old Testament any differently than their contemporaries. See Richard Longenecker's *Biblical Exegesis in the Apostolic Period* (Grand Rapids: Eerdmans, 1999).

[2] Malina and Neyrey, *Portraits of Paul*, 83.

[3] Pilch and Malina, *Handbook of Biblical Social Values*, 115.

[4] Quoted in Ben Witherington, *The Paul Quest* (Downers Grove, IL: IVP, 1998), 94.

[5] The actual number of pilgrims at any given Jewish festival is a matter of discussion. The Jewish historians Josephus claims one festival had nearly three million attendants; modern scholars have been willing to admit that there may have been as many as 500,000. Either number provides Christianity with an ample number of witnesses or potential witnesses.

# *Wishful Thinking*

*John 20:9 For as yet they knew not the scripture, that he must rise again from the dead.*

*Mark 9:10 And they kept that saying with themselves, questioning one with another what the rising from the dead should mean.*

How powerful is the desire to believe? Some critics claim that the disciples of Jesus were so persuaded that Jesus would rise from the dead that they came to *believe* that it actually happened. Perhaps, they say, the disciples saw a person who looked like Jesus, and thought he had been resurrected, and the story grew from there. Or, they were so convinced of Jesus' authority and divinity that they came to imagine that they saw him raised from the dead. Perhaps they even suffered hallucinations of a resurrected Jesus. So great was the desire of these deeply religious men (in less polite terms, some would say, "fanatics") that they merely *imagined* the fulfillment of their greatest hopes.

The scenario described has a fatal flaw, however: If we are to believe the Gospels, the disciples were not expecting Jesus to be resurrected at all. There was no wish fulfillment because there was no wish to be fulfilled.

The disciples had no conception in their religious background for the resurrection of Jesus. As we explained in Chapter 3, the Jews of the New Testament era believed that there would be a general resurrection of all men at the time of final judgment, but the idea of the resurrection of a single person prior to that time was never conceived. A unique resurrection before the end of the age would have implied that something was amiss with God's timetable.

The Gospel of John (20:9) presents us with an interpretive puzzle. John and Peter see that the body of Jesus has disappeared. They also see that the graveclothes remain. John *believes*. Yet we are also told, "as yet they knew not the scripture, that he must rise again from the dead." If John did not know that Jesus would rise from the dead, then what was he believing? An even deeper puzzle: After the resurrection had taken place, we see examples of doubt by the disciples (Luke 24:11, John 20:24), which seem out of sync with what we read elsewhere in the Gospels. Didn't Jesus clearly predict that he would rise from the dead (e.g., Matthew 16:21, 17:22-23; 20:18-19; Mark 9:31; Luke 18:33)? Didn't even Jesus' enemies know he had predicted his Resurrection, and isn't that why they wanted guards around the tomb (Matthew

28:62-64), in order to prevent the theft of the body and a claim of a resurrection?

The answer to both of these puzzles rests in the same place. The disciples were *not* expecting a resurrection, but they *were* expecting something else that would remove the body and vindicate Jesus. What were they expecting? Some clues can be gathered by looking at the words used by Jesus to predict his triumphant return from the dead.

The four Gospels use two different Greek words to refer to Jesus' resurrection. The first of these is *anistemi*. This word is commonly used for anyone just getting up from their place. (Matthew 9:9 And he *arose*, and followed him.) The second word that is used is *egeiro*. This means to *be roused*, or *woken up,* usually from sickness, but also from death. (Matthew 8:15 And he touched her hand, and the fever left her: and she *arose*, and ministered unto them.)

Both *anistemi* and *egeiro* are verbs. A noun form of *anistemi*, the word *anastasis*, is used to refer specifically to resurrection. It is used to describe what the Sadducees do not believe in (Matthew 22:23, Mark 12:18, Luke 20:27), and the final resurrection believed in by others in Judaism (Luke 14:14; John 5:29, 11:24).

The word *anastasis* is used to describe the resurrection of Jesus outside of the Gospels. It is used several times in the book of Acts, and is used by Paul, Peter, and the author of Hebrews. These writers also use *anistemi* and *egeiro* of the resurrection of Jesus.

With this in mind, we may now return to our first question: How could John have "believed," yet also not understood about the resurrection? Because he, and the other apostles, and everyone else (including the chief priests) were not expecting a *resurrection*: They were expecting (or for the priests, expecting a claim of) a "raising up" of the body of Jesus: either after the manner of Elijah or Enoch in the Old Testament, or as an exaltation to heaven like the Son of Man in Daniel 7 (a figure with whom Jesus explicitly identified himself), or in extra-Biblical Jewish tradition, an assumption of the body to heaven like that of Moses'. This would have been a sign that Jesus had been vindicated by God. Thus we see how it is that the disciples, when told Jesus would rise after death, "understood not that saying" (Mark 9:32; cf. Luke 9:45) and questioned its meaning (Mark 9:10), and were dismayed, rather than overjoyed, to hear his predictions of death and rising (Matthew 16:21-23). Thus also we see why the enemies of Jesus still wanted the tomb guarded from theft of the body, and why Jesus had to tell Mary, "I have not yet ascended to the Father," (John 20:17), and why the disciples thought they were seeing a spirit (Luke 24:37-8). All parties knew that Jesus had predicted that his body would be missing. What they didn't understand was the *mechanism* whereby the body would disappear, because there was no room in their belief system for a specific resurrection prior to the general one. They knew that Jesus was going, but did not realize that he was coming back so soon, or how he was going to return. [1]

The proposition that the disciples suffered from a bad case of "wishful thinking" stumbles on yet another point. While there was no room within Judaism for an idea that a single person would be resurrected prior to the final judgment, there would be room for another kind of belief, one that we see expressed in a different context: "And when she knew Peter's voice, she opened not the gate for gladness, but ran in, and told how Peter stood before the gate. And they said unto her, Thou art mad. But she constantly affirmed that it was even so. Then said they, It is his angel." (Acts 12:14-15) In Luke 24:37-8, the disciples at first mistake the resurrected Jesus for a spirit. The Talmud, a collection of Jewish commentary material from after the time of the New Testament, records a belief in guardian angels who would assume the appearance of the person they were assigned to protect.[2] If the disciples had seen a person who looked like Jesus, or had visions of Jesus, then they would have assumed that it was Jesus' "guardian angel," not that it was Jesus himself appearing.

There was therefore no resurrection wish to be fulfilled in the minds of the disciples, and no source for a hallucination. The behavior of the disciples, and the claims of the post-resurrection appearances of Jesus, cannot be explained away as the imagination of religious fanatics.

## Notes

[1] The only verses which might be understood to clearly indicate a physical return of Jesus are Matthew 26:32 and Mark 14:28, "But after I am risen again, I will go before you into Galilee." However, the disciples could have easily understood this in terms of spiritual leadership, as in John 10:4, "And when

he putteth forth his own sheep, he goeth before them, and the sheep follow him: for they know his voice."

[2] For this point, see Simon J. Kistemaker, *Exposition of the Acts of the Apostles* (Grand Rapids: Baker, 1990), 441; Ernst Haenchen, *The Acts of the Apostles* (Oxford: Basil Blackwell, 1971), 385.

# *Survival Game*

*Matthew 8:22b Let the dead bury their dead.*

In our next chapters, we will have a closer look at some typical alternative explanations for the Resurrection of Jesus, and examine them in light of the evidence and in light of the social factors we have explored in previous chapters. One of these alternative explanations may seem too ludicrous to pursue: The idea that Jesus never actually died on the cross, but merely fainted away or "swooned," and later revived in the tomb, eventually appearing to his disciples and convincing them that he had been resurrected. By all accounts this absurd theory should have itself died many deaths by this time, but incredibly, skeptics of Christianity continue to revive it and parade it around, just as they suppose Jesus to have been revived.

Typically, the "swoon theory" argument begins by asking what evidence we have that Jesus was dead on the cross. There were no doctors present to certify his death, and only Roman soldiers were there to make an assessment. How then can we be sure Jesus was dead, based on the affirmation of one centurion and perhaps some soldiers, with no training in diagnostics and no modern medical knowledge?

But did the attending Romans really need training in diagnostics or medicine to know that Jesus was dead? Would those who subsequently took charge of Jesus' body (Joseph of Arimathea and whatever retinue he may have had) need such training? No, they didn't. In the ancient world, there was no need for a doctor to certify that Jesus was dead. A pair of good eyes and experience would have been enough. Death today is a clean process. Our doctors certify the dead, and their bodies are whisked away before we have time for more than a glance, and barring unusual circumstances, we see them next in the funeral home "looking natural". This was not the case among the ancients, for whom, except for the very rich, death was an in-your-face experience. Roman soldiers worked the battlefields and enforced the judgments of death. As noted in Chapter 1, the Romans were known to have crucified hundreds, sometimes thousands, of people at one time. Crucifixion victims were affixed to and undone from their cross not with machines, but *by hand.* Everyday persons watched as relatives and neighbors lived, and died, and they took care of the body when death claimed its grisly reward. A third of live births were dead by age six; 60% of all people died by their mid-teens, and only 3% survived to their sixties. So could the Romans have made a "qualified" pronouncement? Could they indeed have had enough "experience" to know when a body was dead? Absolutely.

There are certain clear, immediate or early signs of death that the ancients would have been intimately familiar with. Many of these signs are not familiar to us today, because we never see them unless our profession is that of a medical worker or a coroner.

The first sign we may note is *algor mortis*, or the absence of body heat. After the heart stops pumping, the blood which keeps our body temperature at a warm 98.6 degrees Farenheit stops. The body slowly falls to room temperature over the next several hours. The body's surface will cool immediately; deep organs may require two to three hours to cool. Jesus' body would have been in the possession of several people over the next few hours after the Crucifixion who would not be able to help but notice the decrease in body temperature.[1]

A second sign is *rigor mortis*, or the hardening of muscle cells that begins shortly after death. Just after death, the muscles may be loose, so that, for example, the jaw drops open. Typically rigor mortis may be detectable in 1-4 hours in the face, and in 4-6 hours in the limbs. The stiffening continues until about 6-12 hours following death. The body of Jesus was in the possession of the Romans and/or Joseph of Arimathea long enough to detect the earliest signs of this change in the body. The stiffening of the limbs would have been most noticeable as the body of Jesus was being prepared for burial.[2]

A third sign of death is *livor mortis,* or discoloration due to blood settling after the heart stops. This usually occurs in one and a half to two hours, well within the time when Jesus' body would be in the possession of the Romans and Joseph. Maximum coloration takes between 8-12 hours as the body turns reddish purple to purple due to the accumulation of blood in the small vessels. At the same time, "bleached" or whitened areas appear due to compression of vessels by the body's weight, which stops blood accumulation in the places under pressure.[3]

A fourth sign is *dessication,* or the loss of moisture from the eyes and other moist membranes that gradually take on a burnt look as fluids fail to be replenished. Jesus' eyes would have immediately stopped producing fluid, and internal mucous membranes would have begun to dry out. A fifth sign, which may have particular relevance for the case of Jesus, is the "death rattle." As the brain ceases to control the body, the air in the lungs is expelled, like an inflated balloon being released to fly around a room. At the same time, control of the upper airway would cease, causing partial obstruction of the airway. As the air passes out, the observer hears what is essentially a reverse snore. The tongue flaps as the air is expelled. Not all dying persons have a death rattle but Jesus would have been very likely to have one. The agony of the crucifixion would have led to very labored breathing and the transition from this to a flaccid state when "he breathed his last" would be quite dramatic.[4]

Clearly, none of these conditions required any training in diagnostics to observe. They would have been familiar sights and conditions to soldiers and "men on the street" alike in the ancient world. These signs provide ample, reliable ways of checking for life in a person who appeared to be dead. Death was not something the Romans only saw on television!

Despite these clear signs, some critics have argued that it is possible, and it has been recorded, for people to be mistaken for dead and even to have been buried alive. The few case histories offered, however, only tend to prove that Jesus must have been dead when taken down from the cross. Some accounts of persons being misdiagnosed as dead are clearly apocryphal or untrustworthy. The ancient writer Pliny the Elder, who wrote about 40 years after Jesus' death, collected some stories of people who were taken to be dead even through their funeral, only to awaken just as their bodies were about to be set aflame on the funeral pyre. Whatever credence one might grant these accounts, however, is surely lessened if not destroyed by Pliny's overall tendency to report other obvious absurdities as fact. Among the interesting reports Pliny offers are of races of people who have their feet on backwards and run very fast; can cure snake bites by touch; are androgynous, having a woman's breast on one side and a male breast on the other; have but one leg, and a large foot usable as an umbrella; and have the heads of dogs and communicate by barking. Pliny also mentions a snake so deadly that it can kill a man on a horse if the man touches it with its lance — and it kills the horse, too!

More careful Skeptics may point to examples of modern misdiagnosed deaths. In 1989 in Springfield, Ohio, and in 1994 in San Leandro, California,[5] there were reported cases of persons who were mistakenly taken for dead. The specifics of the cases, however, only reinforce the likelihood that Jesus was dead, and easily identified as dead. The subject of the Springfield case was a blind woman named Carrie Stringfellow, aged 87, who was mistaken for dead at a nursing home and brought to be embalmed. Note again that in modern times, in which death is a sanitized process, there is no reason to think that a nursing home worker would have been informed enough to detect the signs of death. Not surprisingly, legal action was later brought against the nursing home. A newspaper article reported:

> *A mortician said he had been called to pick up Stringfellow at the home. She appeared to be dead, he said. Stringfellow was taken to the hospital after her murmurings startled the mortician, who had been preparing to embalm her at the funeral home. Dr. Sajjad Siddiqi of Mercy Medical Center said Stringfellow was stable and fully alert when she was brought to the hospital...Siddiqi said medical tests had failed to pinpoint what led to the condition that made her appear to be dead. He said he believed she might have suffered a temporary heart blockage that caused her to lose consciousness for several minutes.*

So we have an apparently incompetent nursing home worker, and a mortician who was still preparing for the embalming process when Stringfellow awoke, and had not yet had the opportunity to check her condition. Is this to be compared to soldiers and persons who lived with death on a daily basis, who handled the body of the deceased, and who had a job to make *sure* a person was dead? No, it is what we would expect when death has become sanitized, and in a society where we have grown up watching cartoon characters who can get up with no more than stars around their heads after dozens of deathly stunts. We do not know death as well today. Even if we sit in the hospice with our dying, we seldom or never see rigor mortis develop or the skin discolor. The experts take the body away so that our beloved look lifelike in their coffins at the closing ceremonies. Little wonder death was misdiagnosed in the Stringfellow case!

The example from San Leandro is no more helpful for a Skeptical argument. Here is how the newspaper report put it:

> *An 82-year-old man was found stiff and cold on his bedroom floor and authorities thought he was dead - until he gasped faintly at the flash of a coroner's camera. Frederic Green was in critical condition Friday in the intensive care unit at San Leandro Hospital, said spokeswoman Barbara Maroni. Doctors believe he had suffered a stroke, she said. A neighbor called police after noticing two weeks of mail and newspapers outside Green's door. Officers found Green on the floor Wednesday evening.*

> *He did not appear to be breathing, and his flesh felt hard and chilled. The coroner was called, and "as the technician's camera flashed, there was a very soft gasp or other slight sign of life," Lt. Dennis Glover said.*

Police officers apparently did make an examination, and found what appeared to be rigor and/or algor mortis, but nothing else. Police admittedly should have some experience with death, but detailed examination of the deceased is usually left to forensic experts, whereas police will tend to keep "hands off" until potential crime scene evidence can be evaluated. We do not know how many dead persons the officers had encountered in their careers, versus ancient persons who knew the subject well.

However, let us now consider the argument that Jesus may have been in a state comparable to these persons. If so, then the evidence suggests that Jesus should have been easily recognized to still be alive. Carrie Stringfellow awakened from her seemingly deathly state, apparently on her own. Frederic Green was roused by the flash of a coroner's camera. Jesus was surrounded by stimuli of equal or greater magnitude after being taken down from the cross: The pain of having nails pulled from his arms and legs; being carried down from the cross; being carried around in the elements, and being prepared for burial. If his condition was not as serious (which is quite unlikely), then why would he not have awakened or shown some sign as these people did? If his condition was more serious, then he would have died within moments or hours anyway, or remained in a comatose state. Skeptics must posit a state of health just bad enough not to be woken up by surrounding stimuli, but just good enough to be able to escape the tomb and appear to the disciples as a perfectly healthy, resurrected man, all within a period of less than 40 hours. There is no chance at all that Jesus was unintentionally buried alive.[6]

But is it possible that Jesus was *intentionally* left alive and buried as part of some conspiracy? A related argument suggests that the sponge lifted to Jesus' lips to quell his thirst (Matt. 27:48, Mark 15:36, John 19:29) contained drugs to render Jesus unconscious. On this matter I consulted a physician who is an anesthesiologist with several years of experience in the administration and use of drugs that would cause unconsciousness. He said, "There are modern drugs which, when touched briefly to a mucous membrane will cause death. Other drugs will cause an anesthetic state by a similar action. But none of them existed in Jesus' day, and it is not possible for them to cause the immediate expiration recorded in scripture...Further, John's account notes that 'a jar full of sour wine was standing there' (John 19:29). This was not a jar brought by the friends of Jesus, but by the Romans, further reducing the already impossible chance of drugging Jesus to simulate his death."[7]

Let us grant, though, for the sake of argument, the idea that Jesus survived the Crucifixion (whether intentionally or otherwise) and remained alive in the tomb. Would he be able to push the one-ton stone away and make an appearance? It is not even a remote possibility. One simply does not move a one-ton stone alone, especially someone who had had nothing to eat for at least 20-40 hours, nothing to drink in that same time other than a bit of sour vinegar (it is impossible for someone to go this long with this little water and still have any strength to speak of, especially after loss of blood from flogging), then lain out shivering and losing energy in a tomb with a temperature as low as 56 degrees, and this after hanging for hours on a cross with dislocated shoulders and strained muscles that would be unable to push open a door, much less a one-ton stone. Add to that the idea that this was someone who was supposedly drugged just enough to simulate death, but little enough to recover within the right time as well, and we are left with an example of blind faith in the remotest of impossibilities.[8] A person in such a condition would be, at the very most, rolling not a stone from the entrance to the tomb, but their own body onto the floor of the tomb, where they will expire just as readily as otherwise.

Finally, we may note the certification of death offered by John's Gospel: "But one of the soldiers with a spear pierced his side, and forthwith came there out blood and water." (John 19:34) . Historically, the piercing of a crucified victim was a known way to check for death.[9] There is only one physical circumstance which fits both this story as given and medical science, and that is the one where a patient has died and the blood in his heart has pooled long enough to break into packed cells and serum. A spear thrust into the heart would allow these fluids to pour out with exactly the appearance recorded by John, and in such cases, the patient would be dead.[10]

In short, the theory that Jesus did not die on the cross is completely without merit and contrary to all available textual, medical, and historical evidence. That this absurd thesis nevertheless survives in some circles is strong testimony to the inability of critics to refute the truth of Christianity on more rational grounds.

## Notes

[1] Bernard Knight, *Simpson's Forensic Medicine* (New York: Oxford University Press, 1997), 23-24.

[2] Ibid., 20-22.

[3] Dominick J. DiMaio and Vincent J. M. DiMaio, *Forensic Pathology* (New York: Elsevier Science Publishing, 1989), 21-2.

[4] Consultation with Dr. Ted Noel, Florida Hospital, January 10, 2002.

[5] "Woman, Nearly Embalmed, Leaves Hospital." *St. Louis Post-Dispatch*, Aug. 17, 1989, pg. 2A; *Orlando Sentinel*, Jan. 29, 1994, pg. A20.

[6] In a thorough study of such cases, author Jan Bondesen concludes that the number of verified cases of persons actually buried alive can be counted on a pair of hands. In many cases a premature burial was stopped by an outward sign from the supposedly deceased, and were within the context of more modern times when death became more sanitary. See Jan Bondesen, *Buried Alive: The Terrifying History of Our Most Primal Fear* (New York: W. W. Norton and Company, 2001).

[7] Conversation with Dr. Noel.

[8] Dr. Noel adds: "Most drugs have half lives of less than 8 hours. A drug to simulate death, however, would be a toxin. There are a number of naturally occurring toxins: tetrodotoxin, tetanus, botulinum, and curare. Unfortunately, a dose large enough to create the illusion of death is fatal. The mechanisms are different, but there is no question, they all kill...[and there is the] impossibility of him getting enough drug. He identified the taste and refused. Only the toxins can be effective after that small a dose, and they contradict the thesis by killing Jesus."

[9] The ancient writer Quintilian (*Declamationes* 6.9) reports, "As for those who die on the cross, the executioner does not forbid the burying of those who have been *pierced*." Raymond Brown, *The Death of the Messiah* (New York: Doubleday, 1994), 1177.

[10] Conversation with Dr. Noel.

# *Body Snatchers*

*Matthew 28:13 Say ye, His disciples came by night, and stole him away while we slept.*

If the disciples were not hallucinating or imagining a Risen Jesus, and if there is no chance that Jesus actually survived the Crucifixion, then what is left to propose? Someone had the body of Jesus, and if it was not removed by the life-restoring power of God the Father, then clearly, one must propose a responsible party. Putting together a lineup of potential suspects, however, is not as easy as we might imagine.

**Suspect #1: The Followers of Jesus.** The original "anti-apologetic" to the claims of Christianity was the resort of the Jewish leaders noted above: The disciples stole the body while those watching the tomb were asleep. The disciples, of course, would be prime suspects in such a case, but the standard reply offered to this argument, that the disciples would not have been able to preach, and suffer for, a lie, is substantially confirmed by the social context of the first century which has been outlined in previous chapters. The disciples were in a position in which their claims would be subjected to scrutiny (if they were not dismissed outright) because of their suspicious and exceptional claims concerning the honor of Jesus, and their preaching would have resulted in social and personal sanctions that the ancients would have found intolerable (like being cut off from family), and in extreme cases, martyrdom. They did not preach their message in secret, but in the major urban centers where the two parties with the greatest ability to check their claims — the urban wealthy who had the means to travel and investigate, and the Diaspora Jews who returned to Jerusalem regularly for festivals — were built-in fact checkers stationed around the Empire who could say or do something about all of the historical claims central to Christianity: A triumphal entry into Jerusalem in blatant fulfillment of Messianic prophecy; an earthquake, a darkness at midday, the temple curtain torn in two; an execution, a claim of an empty tomb, people falling out of a house speaking in tongues; healings of illnesses and dysfunctions, and even reversals of death. All of these events took place in public venues. Christianity was highly vulnerable to inspection and disproof on innumerable points, any one of which, had they failed to prove out, would have snowballed into further doubt about the movement's veracity. Making such bold and audacious claims is not the way to start a false religion. One starts such a religion by linking events to obscure *and* nameless people. One does not claim to have healed the daughter of a synagogue ruler, or to have spoken to a Sanhedrin member, or have encountered a Roman solider who acknowledged your power, and asked you to heal his servant, and one especially does not give their names (Jairus, Nicodemus) or rank (centurion) or place of residence, and make things easier to check. A false religion sticks strictly with encounters with "Joe Smith" or "Mary Rogers" or with no-names like the woman at the well (John 4). Such persons of course would have had to be interacted with anyway, but the point is not their presence, but the presence of those of greater social standing and notice, and the claims attached to them. It is impossible that Christianity thrived and survived while making such audacious claims falsely, and even more incredible to suppose that such claims were made with the full and continuing knowledge that the result in most cases would be rejection, ostracization, and persecution.

There are two added layers of difficulty for the missionary preaching of the early church, and they are related to the social prejudices we outlined in Chapter 2. Christianity's prime witnesses to the empty tomb and the Resurrection were from classes of person that were regarded as the most untrustworthy and unintelligent members of society. If Christianity wanted to succeed, it should never have admitted that women were the first to discover the empty tomb or the first to see the Risen Jesus. It also never should have admitted that women were main supporters (Luke 8:3) or lead converts (Acts 16) in the movement. Women were regarded as "bad witnesses" in the ancient world: "In general Greek and Roman courts excluded as witnesses women, slaves, and children... According to Josephus...[women] are unacceptable because of the 'levity and temerity of their sex.'"[1] Women were regarded as so untrustworthy that they were not even allowed to be witnesses to the rising of the moon as a sign of the beginning of festivals! deSilva also notes that a woman and her words were not regarded as "public property" but were rather to be guarded from strangers. They were expected to speak to and through their husbands.[2] A woman's place was in the home, not on the witness stand, and any woman who took an independent witness was violating the honor code of the ancient world. It would have been much easier to have the male disciples of Jesus, or someone like Cleophas or even Nicodemus, find the tomb first.

However, before we get too distressed by this problem of chauvinism, let us note that it wasn't just women who had a problem. Peter and John were dismissed as incompetent witnesses based on their social standing (Acts 4:13), and this reflects a much larger point of view among the ancients. We have noted the problem of having Jesus hail from Galilee and Nazareth. This was as much of a problem for the disciples, and would have hindered their preaching. The Jews had no trust in such people as Peter and John, if we are to believe later witnesses in the Jewish writings, which referred disparagingly to men such as Peter and John as "people of the land," and said: "...we do not commit testimony to them; we do not accept testimony from them." Though this is a late witness from the Jewish Talmud, it represents an ancient truism also applicable in the ancient world as a whole. Social standing was intimately tied to personal character. Fairly or unfairly, a "country bumpkin" was the last person whose testimony you would believe.

The only apostolic witness who could have gotten around this stigma was Paul. With the likely exception of Matthew (who would have been rejected as a witness on other grounds — namely, that he was a dishonest tax collector!), Paul was the only person among the disciples and witnesses to Jesus' resurrected presence who would not have been dismissed out of hand as an unworthy witness. Significantly, however, Paul did not start any of the three largest churches in the Empire (Rome, Antioch, Jerusalem) and only founded a few of the smaller ones, and he nevertheless had to depend on the witness of the disciples for practically all of his information about the historical Jesus. Paul would not be dismissed as an unworthy witness; rather, the reply to Paul would be, "Paul, thou art beside thyself; much learning doth make thee mad." (Acts 26:24) And of course, Paul was not a disciple of Jesus when the body would have had to be stolen.

Thus, though they are the most obvious candidates to finger in a proposed theft of the body of Jesus, everything about the disciples as perpetrators is all wrong. They gained nothing, and knew they would gain nothing; they voluntarily entered into a difficult process in which they had everything to lose; they managed to convince others that Jesus really had been raised, in spite of the inherently suspicious and untrustworthy nature of their persons from the perspective of their contemporaries. The "best" suspects turn out to be terrible suspects. So who is left?

**Suspect #2: The Authorities.** Far down on the list of suspects to have taken the body of Jesus are the men who held the power, and did have possession of the body of Jesus, at certain stages: the *Roman* authorities, represented by Pilate and his underlings, and the *Jewish* authorities — whether those supposed to be friendly to the Christian movement (like Joseph or Nicodemus) or unfriendly to it (Caiaphas or Annas).

The thesis that either Roman or Jewish authorities took the body falls upon the very simple point that if they did have the body, refuting Christianity would have simply been a matter of authority asserting itself. It would have been enough for the political leaders to say, "We took that man's body, and did such and so."[3] This response would have necessitated a reply from Christian preachers and documents, which is conspicuously absent from the record. Moreover, the response of the leadership would have been perpetuated in later documents attacking Christianity. Because of their great interest in stopping the deviant Christian movement, pagan critics like Celsus, or later Jewish criticisms like those found in the Talmud, would have taken advantage of such an explanation readily, and later Christian writers would have been beholden to defend against it. The silence of the records on this account is inexplicable if the authorities from either ruling party took the body of Jesus.

Some have nevertheless proposed that the body of Jesus was taken by political authorities and either disposed of or removed to another place. Recently, Biblical scholar John Dominic Crossan has tendered the Romans as the likeliest suspect, though not as actual thieves: rather, he argues, the body of Jesus was disposed of in a manner typical of Roman victims of crucifixion, and was thrown into a shallow grave or eaten by wild dogs.[4] Crossan's thesis, however, is riddled with difficulties, not the least of which is accounting for the tradition that Jesus was buried in the tomb of a prominent member of the Sanhedrin like Joseph of Arimathea. This was an audacious claim that was simply too open to question and inspection to have been made lightly, or to have been faked. Judaea was a small territory, and the Sanhedrin was a privileged body with limited membership. Even those who would not have heard of Joseph before, whether at the time of Jesus' burial or 40-70 years later, would have the motive and the ability to find out if such a person existed, and Joseph's own family would be ready to confirm (or disconfirm) the burial, and would have the motives to do so: that is, controlling the deviant Christian movement.

Crossan posits a creative answer to this dilemma, and supposes that it would not be difficult to invent a Joseph of Arimathea, or to merely use his name, as it were, picked out of a hat.[5] He notes an incident involving a short story, by modern author Jorge Luis Borges, entitled "The Aleph." The subject of the story is a mysterious artifact that somehow contains all places on earth simultaneously. Borges located this fictitious object in "a house on Garay Street in Buenos Aires." Garay Street, like the Aleph, was a creation of Borges and did not exist in the real city of Buenos Aries. Crossan relates the following account from Borges:

> *"Once, in Madrid, a journalist asked me whether Buenos Aires actually possessed an Aleph." Borges paused, tempted to say yes, until a friend reminded him that such an object would be known worldwide. Borges therefore replied that there was no such thing. "Ah," said the journalist, "so the entire thing is your invention. I thought it was true because you gave the name of the street."*

Thus, Crossan echoes Borges, "The naming of streets is not much of a feat," and he adds, "...if you create the events, why not create names as well?" His conclusion: The apostles could have, rather easily, invented a Joseph of Arimathea and gotten away with it.

Crossan's amusing anecdote, however, only supports our contention that it would have been impossible to invent or misuse a man like Joseph of Arimathea. Borges was questioned here by only *one* journalist, evidently an extremely peculiar one who could not discern fiction from reality, since he believed an item like the Aleph actually could exist and somehow escape being noticed or announced worldwide! On the other hand, the apostles made the claim of the burial in Joseph's tomb and of the resurrection, and it was accepted by *thousands* of people, of varying intelligences and backgrounds. The apostles also went out preaching the resurrection all over the Roman Empire. Borges sold his books around the world, but "The Aleph" was not a unique, singular, and heavily evangelistic claim made in public squares. There is a big difference here in the way that the news was spread.

Next, the journalist in question was in *Madrid,* an ocean away from Buenos Aires. The apostles made their claims in the very backyard of the events they described. It is harder to make up something like this when people who could know better are right at hand. Certainly no journalists in Buenos Aires, no matter how peculiar they were, would have posed such a question as the Madrid journalist did.

Finally, the apostles had powerful enemies (the Jewish leadership) who would have the means, and most definitely the motive, to question their account, and the people of the Empire as a whole, as we have seen, would have been hostile to the message of Christianity. Borges has no enemies of this sort, and the journalist was not his enemy. There was no reason for anyone to actively seek to discredit Borges' story (for that matter, there were few, if any, who would have had reason to take it as a true story to begin with). In summary, there is an enormous difference between making a claim about a single street in a large metropolitan city and making a claim about the existence and doings of a major (and wealthy) political figure connected with a controversial and socially undesirable movement. Crossan's parallel is irrelevant and inadequate.[6]

**Suspect #3: Whoever is Left!** After the disciples, and the authorities, who remains as a suspect? To those who desire to avoid the conclusion that the Resurrection actually occurred, it seems, any candidate is handy, even if there is no record of them at all. One prominent skeptic of Christianity has seriously suggested that Jesus' tomb was pilfered by occultists seeking the skull of a "holy man" with which to practice their evil arts. There is no evidence, however, for such activity in Judaea, and such tomb robbers usually sliced what they needed off of the body (a nose, or an ear) and left the rest of it behind. Yet another has proposed that Jesus had an otherwise unknown identical twin who took the body, then impersonated the resurrected Jesus! That skeptics must resort to such soap opera scenarios as explanations testifies to the inescapable conclusion that the data, *as it stands*, shows that the Resurrection is the only viable explanation for the missing body of Jesus.[7]

## Notes

[1] Malina and Neyrey, *Portraits of Paul*, 82.

[2] deSilva, *Honor, Patronage, Kinship and Purity*, 33.

[3] It would not have been necessary, as some have proposed, for the Jewish or Roman leaders to remove the body of Jesus from the tomb and wheel it through the streets of Jerusalem. Such an act would have deeply offended the average Jew even if it did prove a point. The authority of the Sanhedrin or of Rome would have been an imposing enough barrier for the Christian faith.

[4] John Dominic Crossan, *Who Killed Jesus?* (San Francisco: HarperCollins, 1995), 160-88.

[5] Ibid., 176.

[6] Moreover, Byron McCane has shown that Crossan's thesis is contrary to what we know about both Roman and Jewish practices and concerns: "Based on what we know of Jewish culture, [the Jewish leaders] would have preferred for Jesus to be buried, and promptly." McCane, "Where No One Had Yet Been Laid," 437.

[7] To demonstrate this point, I have purposely excluded the argument that Matthew indicates that the tomb was *guarded* (Matt. 27-64-6), which makes a theft by any party at all even more impossible. However, even without the guard specified by Matthew, the Jewish authorities would undoubtedly have called upon their reserve of Temple functionaries — of whom they had several thousand — to stand watch on the tomb, even if from a distance, and report suspicious activity. Furthermore, it would have been in their best interests to watch the tomb in order to prevent mourning (which was seen as a way of restoring honor to the dead).

# *Conclusion:*

# *The Impossible Faith*

*Acts 2:37 Now when they heard this, they were pricked in their heart, and said unto Peter and to the rest of the apostles, Men and brethren, what shall we do?*

If what we have presented here is true; if Jesus Christ truly rose from the dead, and if the rise of Christianity is explicable by no other means than the Resurrection, a challenge lies before each person reading this book. An event of earth-shattering proportions, one that in some way affects the lives of every person who lives, who has lived, or ever will live, took place just outside Jerusalem at some time approximately 1970 years in the past. We cannot ignore the implications of the Resurrection. The evidence stands before us, awaiting our decision. We will either accept it, attempt to refute it, or do what we can to pretend that it doesn't matter.

As a whole, we will find that either the second or third reaction, or a combination thereof, will be the likeliest responses to these arguments from those not willing to accept their implications. Christian author Lee Strobel has told us of a time when he was an atheist and his newborn daughter was diagnosed with a life-threatening illness. Though he was an atheist, he tells us, he "was so desperate" that he "actually prayed and implored God — if he existed — to heal her. A short time later, she astounded everyone by suddenly getting completely better. The doctors were left scratching their heads."[1] Yet Strobel did not become a believer in God that day. His response was "to explain it away" as some sort of coincidence. As he goes on to say, "I wouldn't even consider the possibility that God had acted. Instead, I stayed in my atheism...Even if there had been a proliferation of corroborating evidence that God had intervened, I would have come up with any explanation — no matter how bizarre, no matter how nonsensical — other than the possibility that [God] had answered my prayer. I was too proud to bend the knee to anyone, and too enmeshed in my immoral lifestyle to want to give it up."[2]

Strobel rounds off this confession rather poignantly: He knew that, had he wished to do so, the words of the experts he interviewed for his books (*The Case for Christ, The Case for Faith*), experts who provided solid and enduring testimony of the validity of the Christian faith, he could, if he so desired as an atheist, have continued to explain away, "no matter how outlandish or nitpicking my arguments would eventually become. And, believe me, my mind is quite capable of manufacturing all kinds of elaborate rebuttals, excuses, and counter-arguments — even in the face of obvious truth."[3]

When I have previously brought these arguments to the table with others skeptical of Christianity, I have found that Strobel's reaction as a doubter has been repeated a hundred times over. In the Preface, I reported the case of one particular atheist who paid another atheist *several thousand dollars* to write a response to an earlier version of this book. Beyond this, many persons are clearly willing to come up with any explanation, rather than consider the possibility that God has acted in history. One respondent said of an early version of this book, "Still nothing here that refutes my theory that christianity [sic] was the brainchild of a bunch of drunk Roman fratboys out to prove that the unwashed masses would believe anything. Forget proving the existence of god, christians [sic] would go a long way if they would just prove that [Jesus] was an actual person." Another said, "What a ridiculous [argument]. They are basically saying since they don't think Christianity would 'take off'... based souly [sic] on their own opinion, if it wasn't true, then it MUST be true!!" Several others suggested that perhaps the social factors we have described specially lapsed for a while at the time Christianity was founded. The vacuity of these responses is obvious. These are not serious attempts to address the arguments at all; they are, rather, a way to quickly put away the arguments without further consideration. Wild conceptions of Christianity as the invention of drunken Romans, or brushing off the data as a matter of "opinion," is the easy way out. It is our challenge to non-Christian readers to not follow in the steps of these who reject the data out of hand, but rather, to honestly consider the truth of Christianity in this new light as an "impossible faith". To Christian readers, we offer the encouragement of a realization of "how firm a foundation" we have in Christ Jesus.

For more information on this thesis, the reader is welcome to visit <http://www.tektonics.org> or to write the author at jphold@earthlink.net. A prior version of this thesis is found at < http://www.tektonics.org/lp/nowayjose.html > where we offer commentary and responses to criticism.

## Notes

[1] Lee Strobel, *The Case for Faith* (Grand Rapids: Zondervan, 2000), 254.

[2] Ibid., 254-5.

[3] Ibid., 255.

Breinigsville, PA USA
12 March 2010

234101BV00001B/7/A